Bulletin of the
European Communities

Supplement 1/93

Address by Jacques Delors, President of the Commission, to the European Parliament on the occasion of the investiture debate of the new Commission

Strasbourg, 10 February 1993

The Commission's work programme for 1993-94

(SEC(93) 58 final)

The Commission's legislative programme for 1993

(COM(93) 43 final)

Joint declaration on the 1993 legislative programme

EUROPEAN COMMUNITIES

Commission

Cataloguing data can be found at the end of this publication

Luxembourg: Office for Official Publications of the European Communities, 1993

ISBN 92-826-5358-7

© ECSC-EEC-EAEC, Brussels • Luxembourg, 1993

Reproduction authorized

Printed in Belgium

Contents

	Page
Address by Jacques Delors, President of the Commission, to the European Parliament on the occasion of the investiture debate of the new Commission	5
The Commission's work programme for 1993-94	15
I — Introduction	16
II — Internal action	17
III — External action	21
IV — Horizontal action	22
The Commission's legislative programme for 1993	25
Introduction	26
Programme	30
Annexes	48
Joint declaration on the 1993 legislative programme	67

Address by Jacques Delors,
President of the Commission,
to the European Parliament
on the occasion of the investiture debate
of the new Commission

Mr President,
Ladies and gentlemen,

A new Commission comes before you today for the traditional investiture debate. Under the old procedure or the new, the test is the same as far as I am concerned. I am looking forward to your debate and will take a keen interest in your resolutions.

The new Commission's two-year term may seem short, but in these difficult days for European integration, it may prove long enough. The next two years will be crucial, not only for the Community, but for the future of Europe as a whole.

There are many, in government circles in particular, who would like the Commission to be cautious. They will be quick to blame us if we make what might be seen as a false move. There are others, including many members of this House, who feel that we are too timid and want us to be more adventurous. Whatever way you look at it, the Commission is the ideal scapegoat.

All I can say is that both groups might understand these trying times and no longer feel the need for a scapegoat if they were to reflect on the words of the sociologist, Alain Touraine: 'There are those', he wrote, 'who feel that Europe is not very good at projecting its image, but there are more radical reasons than that. We have lived through a decade which saw the overthrow of a series of *anciens régimes* and ultra-liberal illusions. We live with uncertainty and disarray. Life is beginning to sound more and more like a weather report, with its ups and downs, its good days and bad. The irrational has taken over ...' He went on: 'politics are meaningless; anything goes'.

The economy is in crisis, society is in crisis, democracy is foundering. Victims abound, beginning with the unemployed and the dispossessed. And if the trend continues there are other potential losers. The very idea of a united Europe could be in peril.

Let me begin by assuring you that the Commission will not opt for easy solutions or waste its time in self-criticism. Its sense of duty is too strong. And it has good arguments for attempting to reconcile its role as the powerhouse of the Community with the need to respect a body of public opinion that is, quite rightly, questioning the aims and alleged benefits of European integration.

The general malaise of society apart, there are three main reasons for this and, I fear, for our difficulties and your dissatisfaction.

First, with the world-wide economic crisis, Europeans have forgotten the truly impressive advances that flowed from revitalization of the European venture thanks to Parliament's draft constitution, the 1992 target, the boost provided by the Single Act and the 1988 consensus on policy and financial priorities.

But we have run out of steam. What is worse, unemployment is on the increase, spreading to all sectors of the workforce. It is threatening the very fabric of our society, it is jeopardizing the funding of our social protection systems, it is the root cause of the worrying phenomenon of marginalization and exclusion. And the people of Europe are rightly asking: 'Are you, the advocates of a united Europe, capable of coming up with an economic and social programme that will stem the tide of unemployment and restore confidence in the future?'. We must concentrate on answering this question and avoid sterile interinstitutional battles.

Secondly, — and there is a link — the people of Europe woke up when the Treaty on European Union was signed and the ratification process began. It is as if European integration, with all its ups and downs, had made progress up to that point despite the apathy of the public and their elected representatives. European integration was taken for granted in a way. That is no longer true, and I for one welcome the change. As the demand for democracy grows, we must explain, again and again, what we are doing and why. We must reassure the reluctant and encourage the enthusiastic. This is why the old Commission was so keen to put flesh on the bones of the subsidiarity principle. This is why Parliament could play a vital role in these dark days.

The third reason is no secret to this House, which has always been in the vanguard of the campaign for political union and a coherent Community with the means to match its ambitions. It is quite simply that our 12 Member States do not see eye to eye on the fundamental issue of where Europe is going. It is important to remember this. The Maastricht Treaty provides a perfect illustration. The text is based on compromises, often at the expense of clarity and effectiveness. This House has denounced these compromises. It has deplored the opt-outs granted to some Member States and criticized the sterile ambiguity of many articles. But we must not dwell on this for fear of igniting the embers of our disappointment. We must be realistic: we must accept the need to review our institutional structures and our decision-making procedures to make the Community more successful than it has been at reconciling effectiveness, diversity and democracy.

This, then, is the background to the Commission's programme for 1993 and 1994. We will have every opportunity of looking at it in detail with this House and its Committees. With this in mind and on the basis of an analysis of our problems, I would like to launch an in-depth debate today on a number of key questions: how are we to overcome the Community's crisis of confidence? How are we to restore economic and social credibility? How are we to generate political momentum? And how are we to increase the Community's influence abroad?

In the first place, how are we to restore the economic and social credibility that we have undoubtedly lost? Let me begin by taking you back a few years. To 1984, when the Fontainebleau European Council put an end to almost five years of insidious crisis and gave the green light for revitalizing European integration. This was particularly significant at the time, when 'Euro-sclerosis' was a major concern. And then to 1990, by which time pessimism was a thing of the past. Buoyed by the prospect of a single market, the European economy had acquired a new dynamism: growth was strong, investment had increased spectacularly, more than 9 million jobs had been created in six years. From the outside, the Community was admired and feared, which is why 'fortress Europe' replaced the image of a Europe in decline.

As 1993 begins the change of scene is remarkable. Despite progress since 1985, the Community has failed to cushion the effects of the economic crisis within its borders. The crisis has hit it head-on, so much so that the process of ratifying the new Treaty has been dogged by anxiety, by scepticism and, even more importantly, by collective amnesia about past achievements.

The elation of 1990, in the wake of the liberation of Central and Eastern Europe, has given way to depression as the Yugoslavian tragedy casts its shadow.

To be frank, routine cooperation between our 12 countries has weakened in the face of these developments. Can you remember the key idea that was to mobilize our energies and bring us closer together? It was, of course, economic and monetary union. On the stocks since 1988, it presupposed a medium-term economic strategy, based on gradual convergence of our economies, underpinned by the consolidation and the successes of the European Monetary System. In the Commission's view, and in the spirit of the second package of financial and structural measures, the parallel priorities were increased competitiveness and greater economic and social cohesion.

Economic convergence, a stronger European Monetary System, job creation — these priorities, ladies and gentlemen, formed a whole. But they were to be put in jeopardy by a number of factors. Chief among these was the renationalization of economic policies, leading us away from the waymarked path to convergence which was to bring us in stages to economic and monetary union. And they were to be weakened by the European Council's refusal to give the Community the means, in the shape of concerted research and training projects, to encourage European companies to cooperate to become more competitive in a world dominated by economic war.

To put it another way, had the Council of Ministers approved Martin Bangemann's paper on a policy for industry, the European Council would have disavowed the Ministers. Within the limits of its powers and possibilities, the Commission intends to correct the compass reading, as it were, and lead the Community back to the right path. It proposes to reconcile the short-term approach and the medium-term strategy, to take up the economic challenge, to make good the social deficit.

The immediate aim of the European growth initiative is to send a signal. I must warn you that it is not a miracle cure, but rather a reflection of our determination to get out of the doldrums and overcome a 'devil take the hindmost' attitude. The Commission's proposals were approved in Edinburgh. Thanks to Henning Christophersen the Community dimension should be in place within the next few days. But this has to be fleshed out by action at national level using available margins for manoeuvre. This is the purpose of next Monday's meeting of Ministers for Economic and Financial Affairs. So much, then, for the short term.

But we need a medium-term perspective too. This implies turning a deaf ear to the siren voices that tempt us to go it alone, to look after number one, all too often the attitude of governments in times of crisis. If we fail to reverse this trend, our countries will suffer individually, because competitive devaluation is not the answer to the problems facing us today.

History teaches otherwise. As does *de facto* solidarity between the Twelve. An even more serious consequence, however, is that the timetable for economic and monetary union may not be met, with the result that we will lose the hard-won gains of 1985 to 1990.

These are the challenges that, to my mind, should mobilize this House and persuade it to use its influence to get Europe back on track. You know that the Commission is prepared to work closely with you.

The first priority, then, must be to ensure the success of the European growth initiative. This would affirm the need for Community action in areas where it is patently appropriate. Firstly, the development of public investment in infrastructure networks, now generally recognized as vital to the effectiveness of the single market, the modernization of our economies and the development of remote regions. Secondly, the revival of private investment, with the accent on small businesses. Thirdly, selection by the Commission, which has released the necessary funds, of a number of exemplary research projects which, two years from now, could make all the difference to the survival of certain industries. And, fourthly, aid to technological change — provided for by the new Treaty — thanks to programmes to train, retrain and adapt the workforce.

If each Member State adds its contribution, if the expected upturn finally materializes, I am convinced that the Community's economy will find itself back on the road to recovery.

At the same time we must consolidate, not merely defend, the European Monetary System. It may be unfashionable to say so, but the advantages of a system combining more or less fixed exchange rates and macroeconomic cooperation far outweigh the anticipated benefits of a return to floating exchange rates.

Experience since 1979 has proved it. Last week brought a glimmer of hope after months of pussyfooting which have cost us dearly since August. We must persevere, we must confirm our political determination in the face of speculation, we must strengthen economic and monetary cooperation to make our stance credible. I will say no more on this sensitive issue, where recriminations and public pronouncements can have unfortunate consequences. It's a case of least said, soonest mended.

Finally, we must continue to develop the single market and our common policies which have been copper-fastened by a seven-year financial guarantee with the adoption of the second package of structural and financial measures, although the Commission's original proposals, on competitiveness in particular, have been watered down. The Commission has reorganized itself so that it can manage the single market, remove the remaining obstacles, demonstrate the potential of a vast competitive area to the business community, and guarantee full implementation of the four freedoms, including free movement of individuals. Dieter Rogalla will know what I mean.

The common policies offer enormous opportunities in the short and the long term. The reformed agricultural policy gives expression to our acceptance of the demands of world trade. It is now for other countries to make their contribution. The new policy will increase our competitiveness and guarantee our position as a major agricultural power. But it will also ensure the future of all sorts of farms and of farmers themselves, who play such an important role in the development of rural areas. Structural programmes — Objective 5b in our jargon — will make a contribution too.

The Community is also feeling the need for a common environmental policy, the foundations of which have been laid over the years. I realize that the issue is debatable, but the fact of the matter is that the environment is at risk, with dramatic consequences for the future. We must be aware of this and prepare ourselves for the necessary changes in production methods, lifestyles and tax structures. We need to understand that an ambitious environment policy could make a positive contribution to economic and social development and create hundreds of thousands of new jobs.

For the spectre of unemployment hangs over all our achievements, not least our social protection systems and their financing. Under-employment is at the root of many of society's current ills: social exclusion and poverty, the hopelessness of young people and the repercussions of this on the effectiveness of our education systems, the financial cost of unemployment at a time when resources could be channelled to growth and job creation. I cannot claim — nor can the

Commission — to have all the answers. Much depends on national policies and the action taken by businesses and local authorities.

I would stress, however, that the so-called economic and social cohesion policies, implemented under the structural Funds and the new fund set up by the Treaty on European Union — which will become operational in April if the Council gets a move on — have made a useful contribution.

To those who claim that the EMU strategy is deflationary, I would quote three figures. Prior to 1985, an average of ECU 5 billion was allocated to the structural Funds. Between 1988 and 1993, ECU 13 billion was allocated under the first package, and between 1994 and 1999 ECU 25 billion will be made available under the second package. Is this enough to convince people and restore hope? It is far from certain since workers have the impression that 'social Europe' is a mirage. I sympathize with them, as redundancies multiply and the Social Charter remains a pious aspiration. But the Commission is not discouraged. Today, as yesterday, it is pursuing its efforts to breathe life into the social dialogue, the most recent example being consultations with management and labour on the content of the European growth initiative.

The Commission will take up the cudgels again to convince the Council of the value of certain Social Charter proposals which are still on the table — not simply because of the opposition of one Member State. One example is the Directive on the information and consultation of workers in transnational companies. Recent events — but there have been others — have highlighted the confusion and the understandable irritation of employees who have been affected by painful decisions, with no information — as a minimum of respect would require — about the problems and plans of their employers, no opportunity to express their views, and no chance to prepare for a change in their circumstances. In the context of discussions between management and labour — the social dialogue that I have encouraged since 1985 — I also intend to raise the question of workers' access to training throughout their working lives. The right to continuing training is enshrined in the first framework agreement negotiated by management and labour at European level.

The social dimension is the Achilles heel of a Community that is misunderstood, that lacks grassroots support. For the Commission at least the issue is not an ideological one. The social dimension is, quite simply, an integral part of the European venture. It will be kept alive by the social dialogue and the new opportunities opened up by the protocol to the Maastricht Treaty for negotiations between management and labour. But there will be a credibility problem until the Council stops prevaricating and gives concrete expression to the spirit of the Social Charter.

This brings me to the problem of generating political momentum. It is clear that nothing can be done until the Community consolidates its economic base, which is the source of its dynamism or lack of dynamism as the case may be. European union, the stated aim of the Maastricht Treaty, presupposes a carefully conceived, jointly agreed and well-organized economic area. Once Europeans regain their old confidence — and that depends on us — overcome the economic crisis and get back on the road to recovery, they will rally to our collective venture and demonstrate the demand for Europe.

Paradoxically, the demand for Europe from outside the Community is as strong as ever. Witness the growing number of applications for membership. Enlargement negotiations are now officially under way with Austria, Finland and Sweden and negotiations should start with Norway shortly. Incidentally, all these countries, with Iceland and Liechtenstein, belong to the European Economic Area, an idea I floated for the first time in this House in January 1989. It should come into being before the end of the year, leaving our Swiss friends time to think again. At the same time the Commission is now preparing to present its opinions on the membership applications from Malta and Cyprus.

The attention being paid to the south of the Community is not merely symbolic. Apart from the specific problems posed by these two applications, the Community's concern is to strike a fair balance between the north, the east and the south, and at the same time to highlight the Community's presence in the Mediterranean area, beset by political strains and confronted by development problems.

I would like to come back for a moment to the negotiations under way and insist on a point that was clearly made at the Edinburgh European Council: new members will have to acccpt the *acquis communautaire* in its entirety — the whole Union Treaty and nothing but the Union Treaty.

And to those who may find this more surprising in the future than they do today I would say that the opt-outs for the United Kingdom and Denmark were what you might call a long-service bonus.

The Ten are hoping that all the Member States will be able to accept the complete Union Treaty, with all its objectives and attendant obligations, in time. None of us are resigned to what is known as 'variable-geometry Europe'. But in every democracy the voice of the people must be heard. And we must bow to the will of the people and lead the Community in the direction they want. But nothing will weaken our determination to prepare the ground for entry into force of the new Treaty. It will be one of the new Commission's priorities, an act of faith in the future.

The framework formed by the common policies will need to be enlarged and adjusted to allow application of the new arrangements. We will be making a start, in advance of ratification, on the programmes to create an extensive infrastructure network for transport, telecommunications, databanks and vocational training. The Cohesion Fund, once it is operational, will help to implement these programmes in Greece, Ireland, Portugal and Spain.

In another context, the Commission will be redirecting the thrust of its research programmes to make them more selective, and hence more effective, and to target them on competitiveness problems confronting the steel industry, the automotive industry, the electronics industry, computer manufacturers, and so on. Finally, a number of education programmes — Erasmus for instance, which has been an unqualified success — run out at the end of 1994. We will repeat operations that proved successful and combine programmes that were too thinly spread to concentrate our modest resources — which represent a mere 4% of the training and employment budgets of the Member States — on effective action to help workers adjust to technological change, new forms of work organization and the constraints imposed by the new international division of labour.

Another red-letter day will be 1 January 1994, marking the second stage of economic and monetary union. We will work towards this deadline, determined to show that nothing can divert us from our objective of giving the Community a single currency. This will strengthen its hand, allow it to make the most of the large economic area and contribute to a more satisfactory world monetary order. We will have to set up the European Monetary Institute, but we also need to demonstrate that the Twelve are capable of cooperating more closely on macroeconomic policy and enhancing the management and reaction capabilities of the European Monetary System. Let me repeat — the mechanisms of the European Monetary System must be strengthened without delay.

Much remains to be done if the common foreign and security policy is to operate effectively as soon as the new Treaty comes into force.

The Commission — which has made this the portfolio of one of its Members — will shoulder its responsibilities so that it can exercise the right of initiative it shares with the Council and work for the close involvement of Parliament. I would be less than honest if I told you that I was happy with the foreign policy provisions of the new Treaty. Your reaction was the same as mine. The institutional arrangements do not provide an absolute guarantee of effectiveness. But they must be implemented as they stand so that the decision-making process will not be complicated by demarcation disputes or cumbersome interinstitutional structures. The Commission will be presenting proposals to this end in the very near future.

The Commission will also need machinery to deal with justice and home affairs, although these areas are largely a matter for intergovernmental cooperation. A Member of the Commission has been assigned the task of promoting cooperation in this area and initiating a debate within the Council on policies for getting to grips with immigration and the integration of immigrants. May I remind you — with due solemnity — that the Commission's thoughts on these issues have been with the Council for almost two years now and that the European Council decided to put them on the agenda as long ago as 1990?

May I also make the point that there is a clear link, as you know, between immigration problems and freedom of movement within the Community. And it is above all this freedom that Europeans, polled at the end of last year, perceived as the most important aspect of the single market. The Commission will do all in its power to find an early solution that is compatible with the requirements of security and public order.

Speaking of expectations brings me quite naturally to the democratic dimension, though it never ceases to amaze me that some Member

States that find it so easy to ignore the beam in their own eye are preoccupied with the mote in ours ... But I digress. Let us concentrate instead on setting a good example at European level. Democracy, subsidiarity and transparency were the Commission's watchwords for the Lisbon European Council. It made suggestions for bringing the Community closer to its citizens, for making issues and decisions more accessible and easier to understand, leaving it to national authorities to act and implement measures best dealt with at that level.

João Pinheiro will be speaking to you in a few moments about the arrangements the Commission is envisaging for taking the views and desiderata of this House into account — especially when these are expressed by an absolute majority. But with an eye to the next institutional reform, scheduled for January 1996, I feel obliged to point out that, had the 1991 Intergovernmental Conference accepted the Commission's idea — backed by Parliament — of a hierarchy of norms, the subsidiarity principle could have been applied more rationally without raising the fears that some of you share about a watering-down of the Community.

At all events the Commission intends to conduct this crusade for democracy in close cooperation with this House. It will seek a reasonable way of applying subsidiarity to new legislation and existing instruments, of making Community action more transparent, and, as already agreed in principle, working with you on a pertinent communication policy.

We could also work together on the new powers that Parliament has been given: appointment of an ombudsman, committees of inquiry, the co-decision procedure. Your call for the convening of interinstitutional conferences should provide an opportunity for an exchange of views with the Council and lead to binding interinstitutional agreements defining the role and responsibilities of each institution.

The third question, ladies and gentlemen, is how to increase the Community's influence abroad. There are those who are only too happy to revive the spectre of 'Euro-pessimism', having viewed revitalization of the Community with admiration and fear in equal measure. If the Community is to prove them wrong, it must be strong and effective, it must display a new breadth of vision. We all share this ambition. To the business community I would say that the single market has not run out of steam. The simple fact is that the recession has made it well-nigh impossible to predict the future. It is for us to act, to regain the initiative, acknowledging our strengths and our weaknesses. Lester Thurow, in his book *The European House*, has words of reassurance for us when he argues that whatever obstacles it may face, Europe starts from the strongest position on the economic chessboard.

The launching of the European growth initiative is yet another argument in favour of our proposal that an informal meeting of Heads of State or Government of the industrialized nations be organized ahead of the traditional meeting to be chaired by Japan in July. With proper preparation, a meeting of this kind would underline our collective responsibility in the face of world-wide turmoil. It would convey a message of confidence. And it would dissipate the scepticism which thrives on the inability of the leading industrial nations to coordinate their policies and tackle the pressing monetary, financial and trade problems of the day.

Similarly, successful completion of the Uruguay Round would remove the threat of potentially damaging protectionism. A balance must be struck in the concessions to be made and the final compromise must settle the 15 outstanding issues. The fact is that the Community has demonstrated good will and it expects its partners — and the United States in particular — to do the same. But all we have seen so far are threats and unilateral so-called 'retaliatory measures'. This is not the way to reach agreement on a set of binding ground rules.

What I am trying to say is that without economic muscle the Community will be in no position to demonstrate solidarity with countries suffering from internal divisions and underdevelopment, or to exert any influence on world affairs. Its back is to the wall. The emergence of a Greater Europe gives it a compelling reason to act. The name of the game has changed since 1989, instability and uncertainty are growing apace. The toughest, most complex test will be to bring the Yugoslavian tragedy to an end and offer help and cooperation to the six new republics seeking to rebuild a framework for peace, understanding and mutually beneficial relations. The lessons to be learnt from an episode characterized by the vilest attacks on human life and dignity are too numerous to mention here. We have had our say, expressed our regrets, offered criticism and made recommendations. All I know is that public opinion, rightly or wrongly, has castigated the impotence of the Twelve. Given the current situation and the danger of the conflict spiralling out of control, given current discussions within the Security Council, the latest statements by one of our negotiators are interesting. Lord Owen, who, with Cyrus Vance, has deployed his considerable skills and played every card in the diplomatic and political pack, was speaking after President Clinton had given his preliminary reaction. Lord Owen remarked that the United States could not block the only peace plan on the table and at the same time claim that it was unenforceable and that the United States would not participate in any peace-keeping force. The Twelve, need I say, had already endorsed the plan. And I hear now that the United States is to give its assessment and present its proposals in a few hours' time.

The rest of Central and Eastern Europe is engaged in what, happily, is a more peaceful struggle to build a solid democracy and a modern economy. The Community is fully committed to this process and has signed, or is about to sign, Europe Agreements with all the countries concerned. The support pledged under the Phare programme, under which the Community provides 62% of the aid and loans, is another example of its commitment. Denmark, acting in its own right, is seeking to step up political and economic cooperation with Eastern Europe and will be bringing these countries together shortly for a meeting in Copenhagen.

The situation in the former Soviet Union is more worrying: ethnic confrontation and power struggles are adding to the daily toll of suffering and death. It is proving more and more difficult to create the political and administrative structures that would enable the republics to make effective use of foreign aid. Two-thirds of this is provided by the Community, working with other countries and the European Bank for Reconstruction and Development, which is also extremely active in Central and Eastern Europe.

The European Energy Charter, proposed by the Dutch Prime Minister and taken up by the Community, could provide a sound base, a launching pad as it were, for practical cooperation. The final obstacles to agreement should be removed by the end of the year.

I have mentioned our neighbours to the north and the east. But I have not forgotten our neighbours to the south, who sometimes feel neglected. The Community's Mediterranean policy must remain a priority. Our financial contribution already represents 31% of total world aid to the region, and it is set to rise following endorsement by the Council of the Commission's comprehensive plan. New and more ambitious agreements will be negotiated with the Maghreb countries. These should be complemented by horizontal action to demonstrate the global nature of certain problems and to highlight the *de facto* solidarity which binds the countries which border the Mediterranean. I am thinking in particular of the environment, management of marine resources, and cultural exchanges. The Middle East peace talks are another example of the Community's commitment to the region. It has improved its relations with the parties involved. And multilateral discussions to pave the way for a better future are continuing with active Community support in parallel with the search for a political solution. Might this be the time to launch an innovative idea along the lines of the Coal and Steel Treaty that fathered the Community? Why not a water and energy community in the Middle East to cement cooperation between Israel and its Arab neighbours?

So far I have concentrated on policies towards our more immediate neighbours. But I would not like you to think that the Community's responsibilities stop there. At a time when the North-South Dialogue is being forced to differentiate between countries on the move and countries still struggling with underdevelopment, it would be a feather in the Community's cap if it could launch a debate on all aspects of their economic life: monetary policy and interest rates, financing and indebtedness, and trade. Not that the Community and the 12 Member States have any reason to be ashamed of what they have achieved: the Lomé Convention and official development aid (where we account for more than 40%, directly and indirectly, of the world total). But our global aspirations will go out the window if we content ourselves with managing the status quo and do nothing to create a more equitable world economic order. The Commission will certainly give some thought to this, focusing its attention on the serious problems facing sub-Saharan Africa. It is true that the countries of Africa need to put their own house in order. But we must encourage them by stepping up support for the reforms that are needed.

To complete the picture, let me emphasize that the new Commission and its President will work to enhance relations with Central and South America and to clarify cooperation with China, where economic progress has been spectacular. This brings me back to the responsibilities of the major industrial nations. We are linked to them by joint declarations that are, to our mind, spiralling out of control, given current discussions within the Security Council, the latest statements by one of our negotiators are interesting. Lord Owen, who, with Cyrus Vance, has deployed his considerable skills and played every card in the diplomatic and political pack, was speaking after President Clinton had given his preliminary reaction. Lord Owen remarked that the United States could not block the only peace plan on the table and at the same time claim that it was unenforceable and that the United States would not participate in any peace-keeping force. The Twelve, need I say, had already endorsed the plan. And I hear now that the United States is to give its assessment and present its proposals in a few hours' time.

The rest of Central and Eastern Europe is engaged in what, happily, is a more peaceful struggle to build a solid democracy and a modern economy. The Community is fully committed to this process and has signed, or is about to sign, Europe Agreements with all the countries concerned. The support pledged under the Phare programme, under which the Community provides 62% of the aid and loans, is another example of its commitment. Denmark, acting in its own right, is seeking to step up political and economic cooperation with Eastern Europe and will be bringing these countries together shortly for a meeting in Copenhagen.

The situation in the former Soviet Union is more worrying: ethnic confrontation and power struggles are adding to the daily toll of suffering and death. It is proving more and more difficult to create the political and administrative structures that would enable the republics to make effective use of foreign aid. Two-thirds of this is provided by the Community, working with other countries and the European Bank for Reconstruction and Development, which is also extremely active in Central and Eastern Europe.

The European Energy Charter, proposed by the Dutch Prime Minister and taken up by the Community, could provide a sound base, a launching pad as it were, for practical cooperation. The final obstacles to agreement should be removed by the end of the year.

I have mentioned our neighbours to the north and the east. But I have not forgotten our neighbours to the south, who sometimes feel neglected. The Community's Mediterranean policy must remain a priority. Our financial contribution already represents 31% of total world aid to the region, and it is set to rise following endorsement by the Council of the Commission's comprehensive plan. New and more ambitious agreements will be negotiated with the Maghreb countries. These should be complemented by horizontal action to demonstrate the global nature of certain problems and to highlight the *de facto* solidarity which binds the countries which border the Mediterranean. I am thinking in particular of the environment, management of marine resources, and cultural exchanges. The Middle East peace talks are another example of the Community's commitment to the region. It has improved its relations with the parties involved. And multilateral discussions to pave the way for a better future are continuing with active Community support in parallel with the search for a political solution. Might this be the time to launch an innovative idea along the lines of the Coal and Steel Treaty that fathered the Community? Why not a water and energy community in the Middle East to cement cooperation between Israel and its Arab neighbours?

So far I have concentrated on policies towards our more immediate neighbours. But I would not like you to think that the Community's responsibilities stop there. At a time when the North-South Dialogue is being forced to differentiate between countries on the move and countries still struggling with underdevelopment, it would be a feather in the Community's cap if it could launch a debate on all aspects of their economic life: monetary policy and interest rates, financing and indebtedness, and trade. Not that the Community and the 12 Member States have any reason to be ashamed of what they have achieved: the Lomé Convention and official development aid (where we account for more than 40%, directly and indirectly, of the world total). But our global aspirations will go out the window if we content ourselves with managing the status quo and do nothing to create a more equitable world economic order. The Commission will certainly give some thought to this, focusing its attention on the serious problems facing sub-Saharan Africa. It is true that the countries of Africa need to put their own house in order. But we must encourage them by stepping up support for the reforms that are needed.

To complete the picture, let me emphasize that the new Commission and its President will work to enhance relations with Central and South America and to clarify cooperation with China, where economic progress has been spectacular. This brings me back to the responsibilities of the major industrial nations. We are linked to them by joint declarations that are, to our mind,

States that find it so easy to ignore the beam in their own eye are preoccupied with the mote in ours ... But I digress. Let us concentrate instead on setting a good example at European level. Democracy, subsidiarity and transparency were the Commission's watchwords for the Lisbon European Council. It made suggestions for bringing the Community closer to its citizens, for making issues and decisions more accessible and easier to understand, leaving it to national authorities to act and implement measures best dealt with at that level.

João Pinheiro will be speaking to you in a few moments about the arrangements the Commission is envisaging for taking the views and desiderata of this House into account — especially when these are expressed by an absolute majority. But with an eye to the next institutional reform, scheduled for January 1996, I feel obliged to point out that, had the 1991 Intergovernmental Conference accepted the Commission's idea — backed by Parliament — of a hierarchy of norms, the subsidiarity principle could have been applied more rationally without raising the fears that some of you share about a watering-down of the Community.

At all events the Commission intends to conduct this crusade for democracy in close cooperation with this House. It will seek a reasonable way of applying subsidiarity to new legislation and existing instruments, of making Community action more transparent, and, as already agreed in principle, working with you on a pertinent communication policy.

We could also work together on the new powers that Parliament has been given: appointment of an ombudsman, committees of inquiry, the co-decision procedure. Your call for the convening of interinstitutional conferences should provide an opportunity for an exchange of views with the Council and lead to binding interinstitutional agreements defining the role and responsibilities of each institution.

The third question, ladies and gentlemen, is how to increase the Community's influence abroad. There are those who are only too happy to revive the spectre of 'Euro-pessimism', having viewed revitalization of the Community with admiration and fear in equal measure. If the Community is to prove them wrong, it must be strong and effective, it must display a new breadth of vision. We all share this ambition. To the business community I would say that the single market has not run out of steam. The simple fact is that the recession has made it well-nigh impossible to predict the future. It is for us to act, to regain the initiative, acknowledging our strengths and our weaknesses. Lester Thurow, in his book *The European House,* has words of reassurance for us when he argues that whatever obstacles it may face, Europe starts from the strongest position on the economic chessboard.

The launching of the European growth initiative is yet another argument in favour of our proposal that an informal meeting of Heads of State or Government of the industrialized nations be organized ahead of the traditional meeting to be chaired by Japan in July. With proper preparation, a meeting of this kind would underline our collective responsibility in the face of worldwide turmoil. It would convey a message of confidence. And it would dissipate the scepticism which thrives on the inability of the leading industrial nations to coordinate their policies and tackle the pressing monetary, financial and trade problems of the day.

Similarly, successful completion of the Uruguay Round would remove the threat of potentially damaging protectionism. A balance must be struck in the concessions to be made and the final compromise must settle the 15 outstanding issues. The fact is that the Community has demonstrated good will and it expects its partners — and the United States in particular — to do the same. But all we have seen so far are threats and unilateral so-called 'retaliatory measures'. This is not the way to reach agreement on a set of binding ground rules.

What I am trying to say is that without economic muscle the Community will be in no position to demonstrate solidarity with countries suffering from internal divisions and underdevelopment, or to exert any influence on world affairs. Its back is to the wall. The emergence of a Greater Europe gives it a compelling reason to act. The name of the game has changed since 1989, instability and uncertainty are growing apace. The toughest, most complex test will be to bring the Yugoslavian tragedy to an end and offer help and cooperation to the six new republics seeking to rebuild a framework for peace, understanding and mutually beneficial relations. The lessons to be learnt from an episode characterized by the vilest attacks on human life and dignity are too numerous to mention here. We have had our say, expressed our regrets, offered criticism and made recommendations. All I know is that public opinion, rightly or wrongly, has castigated the impotence of the Twelve. Given the current situation and the danger of the conflict of far-reaching political significance, a point worth making as a new President takes the helm in the United States.

In conclusion I would like to assure you that the Commission attaches enormous importance to next year's European elections. I wonder whether, if we pool our efforts, we can manage by then to overcome indifference, speak to Europe's citizens in their own language, offer them a better future and involve them in the challenging venture of creating a united Europe? We must not forget the forces that threaten our joint venture and so much more; the recrudescence, open or disguised, of nationalism, the menace of racism and xenophobia, attacks on the social systems which are the basis of our European model of society.

If we remain aware of these dangers, we can resume our journey. But we must be resolute and open in our dealings. May I suggest another interpretation of openness and transparency? What if we were to stop looking over our shoulders in constant fear of our discussions or our proposals giving offence? What if each institution — the Commission included — and each Member State were to stop contemplating its navel and recognize that a collective challenge calls for a collective response?

The new Commission, aware of the dangers but of its responsibilities too, intends to continue along the road to European integration and plan for the medium term. It intends, in other words, to give Europeans a future to look forward to again.

It is high time, ladies and gentlemen, to sow the seeds of hope.

The Commission's work programme for 1993-94

I — Introduction

1. The framework for the Commission's activities in 1993 and 1994 is already in place. The single market became operational on 1 January and its success will now depend on how it is managed; action will have to be taken on the major political priorities flowing from the European Council's conclusions on the second package of financial and structural measures and the 1993-99 financial perspective; as agreed in Edinburgh, the ground will have to be prepared for implementing the Treaty on European Union once ratification is complete; and enlargement negotiations are about to begin. The Commission will operate within this general framework, attaching special importance to practical measures that will help to improve the Community's image, which was tarnished in 1992. These will include measures to boost the Community's economic performance, to increase openness and improve communications with the general public, to make the frontier-free market operate smoothly and to ensure greater consistency in action taken by the Community abroad.

A new phase of European integration is beginning. It will be dominated by pragmatism, calling for a review of certain activities and solid, visible results in the short term, and by preparations for what lies ahead.

2. Against this general background, the Commission intends to concentrate on four main areas:

(a) The success of the single market is crucial to the Community's credibility. The frontier-free area offers considerable potential for growth and is a vital factor for economic recovery. It is also the most immediate, practical and visible manifestation of what European integration has to offer the businessman, the worker and ordinary citizens. But much remains to be done. The importance of management, monitoring and follow-up and the essential flanking measures and policies cannot be underestimated.

(b) A constant concern must be to concentrate Community action on what is essential or indispensable to attain its objectives. At this juncture it is more important than ever to ensure that there is no wasted effort and that action concentrates on the political and financial priorities that have been set. The next two years will be difficult from the financial point of view following the European Council's decision not to raise the ceiling on the Community's own resources before 1995. Another task for the Commission will be strict but positive application of the principle of subsidiarity. Planned measures will have to be assessed in terms of what would happen if they were not taken or were taken at another level. The Commission will also highlight the benefits to citizens of every measure proposed.

Within the Community the Commission's activities over the next two years will focus on stimulating the economy, strengthening economic and social cohesion and boosting business competitiveness, along the broad lines set out by the European Council. But action outside the Community will be equally important. The key areas will be completion of the Uruguay Round, the opening of accession negotiations and the organization of relations with Central and Eastern Europe. A top priority will be the search for a lasting, peaceful solution to the conflict in what was Yugoslavia. And the deepening of relations with the Community's Mediterranean neighbours and cooperation with the developing world will continue to be a major concern.

(c) The Commission will also make active preparations for implementing the Treaty on European Union as soon as it is ratified. Three main elements have to be considered here.

The first is Stage II of economic and monetary union, made more necessary than ever by the slowdown in economic growth and the recent turmoil on foreign exchange markets. Neither of these factors should be allowed to disrupt or delay progress in laying this vital foundation for the economy of the future union.

At the same time, structural policies must be adapted to the guidelines of the second package of structural and financial measures, and the new Cohesion Fund must become operational without delay.

A second element is a contribution to the launching of a genuine common foreign and security policy as a worthy successor to the political cooperation machinery. In view of the problems confronting the Community abroad everything possible must be done to organize joint action on a scale commensurate with the political, economic and moral responsibilities of the future union. In this context the Commission is reviewing its internal organization and its working methods.

The success of the new Treaty also presupposes efficient organization of work on justice and home affairs. The Commission is ready to make its contribution to appropriate action on immigration based on the proposals it has already made.

Lastly, steps must be taken to ensure the success of the co-decision procedure, which is central to the union's constitution and its democratic credentials.

(d) Information and communication. It became all too clear in the course of 1992 that much needs to be done to improve public awareness and public perceptions of the Community. There are many reasons for this, but it is obvious that steps need to be taken to bridge the qualitative information gap and convey a comprehensible message about the Community and its aims.

The European Council has shown the way. The Commission is determined to play its part, explaining its actions more clearly, providing more information about its work and highlighting the benefits the Community brings to the man in the street.

Once the report of the group of experts appointed to review information and communication policy is available, the Commission will launch a series of initiatives and commit the necessary resources to ensure that the importance it attaches to communication is reflected in administrative action and well-targeted information.

This will be helped by continuation of an active audiovisual policy designed to promote more extensive cultural exchanges which will accentuate the European identity.

3. Given this backdrop and work already in hand, the initiatives planned by the Commission can be grouped under three main headings — internal action, external action and horizontal action. The Commission trusts that the proposals outlined in the pages which follow and in the accompanying legislative programme will provoke a lively debate within the Community's institutions and in the Member States with a view to involving the people of Europe in the development of Community policies.

II — Internal action

Making a success of the frontier-free area

4. Succcess here is imperative. Confidence in the Community depends on it, since businessmen and the general public expect to avail themselves, without let or hindrance, of the four freedoms associated with the single market. Economic success depends on it too, since it is vital to make the most of the potential for growth generated by proper functioning of the large market. The Commission intends to take up this major challenge, paying particular attention to day-to-day management, notably with the installation of a data communications network between government departments, and following up any problems that may arise. It will also see to it that the residual obstacles still awaiting a solution are eliminated without delay.

5. A whole series of practical measures will be necessary if the single market is to operate smoothly and efficiently without placing any excessive burden on firms in general and small firms in particular. To this end, the Commission will keep a close watch on developments and foster dialogue with the Member States along the lines set out in its paper on action to be taken on the Sutherland Report.

6. In addition to these essential management tasks, a number of legislative decisions have still to be taken. To date, 95% of the 282 proposals in the White Paper have been adopted. Tax controls and physical checks have been abolished for all practical purposes. But 18 White Paper proposals — some of them extremely important — are still pending before the Council. They include indirect taxation of certain goods and services (secondhand goods and works of art, passenger transport and gold), road cabotage, and trade in a number of specific products. Unless there is an early decision, this lacuna is bound to create problems for the single market. Furthermore, the business environment would be improved if the outstanding fiscal and legal measures contained in the White Paper (statute of the European company) or subsequent to it (elimination of double taxation and allowances for losses in another Member State) were adopted. Lastly, a number of supplementary proposals have to be presented, dealing with observance of copyright and neighbouring rights.

7. However, the thorniest problem is the abolition of controls on people at the Community's internal frontiers. Delays in ratifying the Dublin Asylum Convention, failure to sign the External Frontiers Convention, ongoing difficulties over the setting up of an information system, but above all persistent differences of opinion on the interpretation of Article 8a of the Treaty, have led to stalemate. The Commission, within the limits of its powers and possibilities, will contribute to an overall strategy to be put in place in 1993 to remedy the situation.

Generating economic momentum

8. The Community must use all the means at its disposal to counter the significant slowdown in economic activity. Its credibility and its very future are at stake. The consequences of this situation are all too obvious and remain unacceptable: growing unemployment, dwindling business confidence, regions stripped of their traditional balance, countries labouring under ever-tighter financial, budgetary and fiscal constraints. The European growth initiative, steps to increase business competitiveness and preparations for Stage II of economic and monetary union are the main levers that the Community can pull to generate economic momentum, mobilize energies and restore confidence.

9. The growth initiative approved by the European Council should promote economic recovery in Europe. For the first time ever, concerted action by the Member States is to be matched by Community action to stimulate growth. The Commission has made its contribution to this novel measure. A raft of measures will have to be adopted without delay. One is the creation of the European Investment Fund, with ECU 2 billion in subscribed capital, which will be used to guarantee investment in infrastructure projects and facilitate loans to small businesses, particularly in less-developed regions. Early steps must also be taken to define arrangements for access to the special loan mechanism to be created within the EIB to finance infrastructure projects, including those associated with trans-European networks.

These financial arrangements must be supplemented as soon as possible by provisions to speed implementation of the single market, to make the Community's research effort more selective, to expand training schemes and to continue providing support for small businesses. The Commission will do all it can to ensure that economic policy concertation is tightened in line with the conclusions of the European Council.

Finally, it will use all its powers and every opportunity for international dialogue to lead its partners along the road to economic recovery, in the light *inter alia* of the approach adopted by the new US Administration.

10. Given the guidelines approved by the European Council, the Commission will pursue its efforts to increase business competitiveness, concentrating on five priorities: development of infrastructure networks, support for research, creation of a favourable environment for small businesses, promotion of fair competition between economic operators, and anticipation of industrial change.

(a) Existing Commission proposals to promote the development of trans-European networks will be supplemented (master plans for traditional railways, air traffic control, ports and airports). The aim here is to promote the interconnection and interoperability of national networks within the frontier-free area and to reinforce links between the centre and remote regions and also between these remote regions. To this end, proposals will be presented on broadband and digital telecommunications networks, natural gas and electricity networks, and the interoperability of the high-speed train networks.

(b) On research and education, the main task, with a view to enhancing the quality and effectiveness of Community action, will be to adapt assistance to the development and real needs of businesses and to the quality of life. For research, a limited number of priority technologies and major scientific projects will be selected. Community involvement must present a real advantage over what has been done at other levels to meet new scientific and technological challenges. For education operations will be mounted under the subsidiarity principle which can help achieve the single market for the professions. The Commission will endeavour to promote these principles and foster cooperation between the Member States in its proposals under the fourth framework programme and the education programmes.

(c) Small businesses are a factor for innovation, performance and flexibility and for this reason are a major contributor to job creation. Because of their enormous potential, the Commission will strive to provide them with a favourable environment. It will propose appropriate guidelines in the light of the results achieved by the enterprise policy measures included in the growth initiative. It will also consider the feasibility of a programme targeted at cooperatives, mutual societies, associations and foundations.

(d) In the area of competition policy, the Commission will continue to adopt a vigilant and constructive approach. Its role will be given a new dimension by the dynamics of the single market. It will have to ensure healthy competition that stimulates business performance, supports the process of change and protects consumers' interests. The Commission will be considering a proposal for revision of certain provisions of the merger control regulation.

(e) Adjustment to industrial change and changes in production systems is one of the keys to competitiveness today; it is also an essential element of social cohesion. For this reason the Commission will be taking practical steps, under the structural policies, to improve training for the workforce and to facilitate redeployment where required. Given the pace of technological change, it is particularly important to tighten links between training and research. The Commission is working along these lines and will be redefining existing programmes (Erasmus, Force, etc.) which expire at the end of 1994.

11. Immediate attention must be given to preparations for Stage II of economic and monetary union, which is due to begin on 1 January 1994. It is of the utmost importance that this objective be met to maintain economic momentum in the long run. The growth initiative is designed to satisfy short-term requirements; strengthening competitiveness will improve the real performance of firms in the medium term; but economic and monetary union will give Europe's economy a stable macroeconomic and monetary framework in the longer term. In accordance with the new Treaty the Commission, as agreed at Edinburgh last December, will be proposing rules in the course of the year to prohibit monetary financing of public deficits, to prohibit privileged access to financial institutions, to apply the protocol on excessive deficits and to establish the European Monetary Institute. It will also present the customary report on convergence.

Strengthening cohesion

12. The new financial perspective agreed in Edinburgh provides for the doubling of assistance to the least prosperous Member States and a substantial increase in other structural operations. This is clear confirmation of the solidarity which underpins the Community. The guidelines laid down by the European Council require action on two fronts: establishment of the new Cohesion Fund and revision of the structural Fund regulations.

(a) The Commission has already proposed arrangements for establishing the Cohesion Fund. It is important that they be adopted without delay. Early agreement must also be reached on the interim legal instrument, which will allow the four eligible countries to receive assistance from the new Fund pending entry into force of the Treaty on European Union.

(b) Proposals for revision of the regulations governing the structural Funds will be made in the very near future to avoid any hiatus between current programming and that covering 1994-99. These proposals will seek to incorporate the structural components of the common fisheries policy and to deal with the problems of areas dependent on fishing. The general approach will be to confirm and reinforce the basic principles of the 1988 reform, namely concentration, programming, partnership, additionality.

Developing the social dimension

13. The Commission is particularly concerned to ensure that the development of action on the social front complies in full with existing rules and objectives and respects the diversity of existing systems, cultures and practices in the Member States. Unfortunately, there has been a serious delay in developing the social dimension of the single market. Many major proposals are still pending, and have been for far too long. One of the priorities for 1993 will be implementation of the programme for giving effect to the Community Charter of the Fundamental Social Rights of Workers and the Commission will endeavour to mobilize the support it needs to improve the results to date. The proposals on the information and consultation of workers in transnational enterprises, the posting of workers and the organization of working time deserve particular attention.

In 1993 too, the Commission will add a few legislative proposals to those already pending. It will seek to add a new dimension to Community action to promote employment and combat marginalization. The Commission will also continue to promote the social dialogue, as it has done since 1985. It will do everything in its power to allow this dialogue to develop in line with the spirit of the agreement signed by the social partners on 31 October 1991.

Lastly, thought will be given to the future with an attempt to chart the future course for Community action in this essential area.

Integrating environmental concerns into other common policies

14. Sustainable development is the primary aim of the fifth environment programme, whose objectives and principles were approved by the

Council on 16 December 1992. At the Rio Summit last June, the international community set itself the same objective, which found expression in Agenda 21, an action programme for the next century. As the first year in which the fifth programme is applied and the objectives set in Rio are pursued, 1993 should see environmental concerns being integrated into the definition and implementation of Community policies in other areas.

As part of this new approach the Commission will be taking a closer look at the economic implications of sustainable development (effects on growth and employment, incorporation of the natural capital into economic analysis, etc.).

Legislation will be needed and major initiatives are planned on matters such as integrated pollution control and environmental impact assessment. Further thought will be given to the question of liability for damage to the environment in accordance with the principle of responsibility for the environment. The Commission will present proposals for revision of the Montreal Protocol on protection of the ozone layer and will monitor progress through the Council of its proposals for measures to implement the strategy for stabilizing CO_2 emissions.

Priority will continue to be given to stricter application of the Community's environment legislation and more effective monitoring of compliance with the rules at national level.

Supporting the single market by other policies

15. Although some measures have been mentioned in a broader context on previous pages, transport policy, energy policy and the protection of consumers' interests deserve particular attention.

16. Infrastructure aside, the political debate on the White Paper on the common transport policy presented by the Commission last December will be extremely important. Priority will be given to two areas: improved safety and closer cooperation with non-member countries, with the replacement of existing bilateral agreements by Community procedures and the extension of transport networks towards Eastern Europe.

17. On energy policy, some basic components of the internal energy market, such as common rules for the markets in electricity and natural gas, have still to be clarified. On the international front, the Commission has already proposed that the Community should accede to the International Energy Agency, but some further adjustments will be necessary. Finally, negotiations will continue in 1993 to allow implementation of the European Energy Charter with the countries of Central and Eastern Europe.

18. The Commission's proposals concerning telecommunications will be designed to establish for a period of 8 to 10 years a stable framework, approved by all interested parties (regulatory authorities, network operators, service suppliers and users), laying down the various measures to be introduced gradually to promote the establishment of advanced trans-European networks. The guidelines for satellite and mobile telecommunciations will continue to be applied. There will be no let-up in the Commission's endeavours to facilitate the introduction of high-definition television in Europe.

19. Most of the Commission's proposals to protest consumers' interests in the single market have been on the table since last year. In its second multiannual action programme, to be presented in 1993, the Commission will place the emphasis on consumer information and consolidation of what has been achieved. It will organize broad consultations, based on Green Papers, on access to the courts and the development of guarantees on financial matters.

Implementing the reform: agriculture and fisheries

20. The reform of the common agricultural policy, which was unanimously considered essential, has been concluded. It will now have to be applied for a first full year in 1993. Flexibility will have to be the principle guiding implementation, with improvements still being possible wherever required, provided the fundamental features of the reform are not compromised.

Coherent arrangements will be adopted for the products not covered by the May 1992 reform which deal with the specific problems and make the market organizations consonant with the outcome of the Uruguay Round. In the final stages of the GATT negotiations the Commission will continue to defend the Community's interests on the agricultural aspects.

Close attention will be paid to the needs of rural development in the reform of the structural Fund regulations.

The reformed agricultural policy will cost ECU 1.6 billion more than forecast as a result of recent movements on the exchange markets. 'Appropriate steps' may have to be taken in due course, as foreshadowed in the European Council's conclusions.

On fisheries, the Commission will be making further proposals for regulations to implement the revised common policy designed to consolidate the new framework regulation and the market regulation with the introduction of a system of licences to reduce catches. Work on establishing common management and conservation arrangements for Mediterranean fisheries will be speeded up and a series of fisheries agreements with non-member countries will be negotiated.

III — External action

21. There are three major challenges here: increasing the consistency of external action by facilitating transition to the common foreign and security policy; preparing for enlargement and organizing new relations with the Community's southern and eastern neighbours; and assuming the world role which befits the Community.

Developing the capacity to speak and act

22. In a world marked by major upheavals, the new framework offered by the second pillar of the Treaty on European Union should give the Community greater political clout and enable it to agree on joint action which is visible, relevant and in the European interest. The allocation of portfolios in the new Commission demonstrates its concern to anticipate the consistency that the common foreign and security policy will provide.

Given the serious problems which have erupted in various parts of the world, not least in Europe itself, it is vital, even in advance of the Treaty entering into force, that the Community make its voice heard and help to find solutions consistent with its traditional values. The Commission cannot close its eyes to the external challenges facing the Community. It is in this spirit, strengthened by its new organization, that the Commission intends to work in the framework of European political cooperation.

The Commission will back developments in this area with proposals for economic and financial cooperation or humanitarian aid.

Preparing for enlargement and improving relations with the Community's neighbours

23. In line with the conclusions of the Edinburgh European Council, accession negotiations are about to begin with Austria, Sweden and Finland. The Commission will produce its opinion on Norway's application for membership and will also give its views on the accession of Malta and Cyprus.

The Commission has already made proposals for the adjustments that will be necessary for implementation of the European Economic Area Agreement.

24. Most of the Commission's proposals for restoring and deepening the Community's relations with the countries of Central and Eastern Europe, the independent States of the former Soviet Union and the Baltic countries are already on the table and internal discussions and negotiations are progressing satisfactorily. The Commission will be presenting further proposals in the course of the year on food aid and environmental protection. It will be implementing the report presented to the Edinburgh European Council, with particular reference to market access. It will seek to improve the organization and enhance the effectiveness and efficiency of technical and financial cooperation with these countries, special attention being paid to assistance in the area of nuclear safety.

25. The agreements already reached on the new Mediterranean policy will enable the Community to step up cooperation with its neighbours to the south. The agreements with the Maghreb countries will be particularly important. The Community will pursue its efforts to contribute to stability in the Middle East through the Peace Conference.

26. The Commission earnestly hopes that current diplomacy will bring to an end the tragedy in what was Yugoslavia. It will take any new initiatives it can to support the people of that war-torn region and help to rebuild the economies of the countries concerned. An economic and financial cooperation agreement with Slovenia will have to be examined by the Council and a request from Croatia for the negotiation of a similar agreement will be studied in 1993.

Acting at world level

27. The joint declarations between the Community and the United States, Canada and Japan form the political and economic framework within which the Community intends to develop its relations and cooperation with these three countries.

The Western Economic Summits should likewise offer the industrialized countries the possibility of stepping up action to assume their responsibilities in the world.

A rapid and balanced conclusion of the Uruguay Round negotiations, which have now returned to a multilateral phase, is vital for the Community's trade relations. It could do much to stimulate activity at a time when so many economic operators are beset by doubt and uncertainty. Once agreement has been reached, a timetable for implementation will have to be prepared.

28. The next two years will bring major challenges for the Community's development policy. Preparations for the new Lomé IV financial protocol will begin in 1993, to be followed by negotiations in 1994. The debate on the paper on development cooperation in the run-up to 2000 should chart the course for this revision, which will set the scene for subsequent changes (Mediterranean protocols, Council guidelines for Latin America and Asia).

Other priorities will include reform of the generalized system of preferences, the Community's financial follow-up to the undertakings given in Rio, the negotiation of commodity agreements for cocoa and coffee and implementation of the Council's guidelines on human rights, democracy and development.

29. The Commission will pay particular attention to the promotion at international level of measures to deal with regional or global environment problems. In line with the undertakings given in Rio, it will launch initiatives and make proposals for saving the tropical forests and ratifying the climate change and biological diversity conventions. It will take part in the negotiations for a convention on desertification and in the work of the UN Commission on sustainable development. It will continue to attach particular importance to protection of the environment in the countries of Central and Eastern Europe and the Mediterranean.

IV — Horizontal action

30. In addition to the priority to be given to information activities, proposals will have to be made on four horizontal issues: subsidiarity, transparency, financing and interinstitutional relations.

Organizing application of the subsidiarity principle

31. On the basis of the memorandum adopted at Edinburgh and in the context of an interinstitutional agreement to be concluded in 1993, the subsidiarity principle will have to be applied not only to new measures but to existing provisions too where the three institutions are in agreement. The Commission intends to make a constructive contribution to the discussions which will be needed to ensure that these guidelines are respected.

Contributing to transparency in a Community closer to its citizens

32. The Commission presented a communication to the Edinburgh European Council on the organization of relations with lobbies (code of conduct, register, broader and more frequent advance consultations). It also tabled an initial contribution to the debate on transparency, dealing with members of the public whose work brings them into contact with the Commission (dissemination of information and consolidation of legal instruments). In addition to implementing the measures set out in these two papers, the Commission will present a second communication on transparency focusing on information policy and relations with the general public.

Providing the necessary financial resources

33. The decision taken by the Edinburgh European Council on the 1993-99 financial perspective outlines the financial framework for the years ahead. An interinstitutional agreement will have to be concluded in 1993 on the basis of this decision. The Commission has just presented the necessary proposals.

Financial and budget constraints dictate the terms of the Commission's administrative management. The Commission will attach continued importance to developing the European public service, which is the guarantee of the effectiveness of its action. The structure of Commission departments and the tasks undertaken by Commission staff will be adapted where necessary to prepare for the future.

Improving interinstitutional relations

34. Interinstitutional practices can be improved in the interests of greater transparency in advance of ratification of the Treaty on European Union. It is important to prepare for what lies ahead and all the opportunities for strengthening democracy offered by the new Treaty should be explored. The Commission will pay particular attention to the most suitable ways of accommodating future developments and will reflect on the organization of its relations with Parliament with specific reference to information, consultation, action on opinions and implementation of the co-decision procedure.

The Commission will make a full contribution to preparing for a rapid and effective installation of the Committee of the Regions.

*
* *

1992 marked a turning point for European integration. The public debate revealed that there is a need for more transparency and clearer explanations of the Community's aims.

This programme seeks to strike a balance over the next two years between concrete achievements and preparations for the future, giving pride of place to economic recovery and international responsibilities. In so doing it hopes to promote a Community true to the principles of solidarity and generosity and closer to its citizens.

The Commission's legislative programme for 1993

THE COMMISSION'S LEGISLATIVE PROGRAMME FOR 1993

(93/C 125/02)

INTRODUCTION

The legislative programme

The legislative programme is a *planning tool* prepared by the Commission of the European Communities to give an overview of the Communities' legislative business. It is *interinstitutional*. Once it has been transmitted to the other institutions and their subordinate bodies have discussed it (Parliamentary Committees, for instance), the programme is adopted by Joint Declaration of the European Parliament, represented by its Enlarged Bureau, and the Commission, in the presence of the Council Presidency.

The objectives of the programme

The programme seeks to attain two primary objectives.

First, it meets a need for *transparency*, that is to say for clear, direct information on the grounds and scheduling of Community legislative business that is pending or foreseeable in the medium term. From 1993, therefore, the programme is to be published in the *Official Journal of the European Communities*. The information it contains is intended both for the Community institutions and for the Member States, the business world and the citizen. The document is also presented in such a way as to improve transparency by distinguishing between planned legislation on which broad consultations could be held in advance and that which might require a business impact assessment.

It also seeks to boost the *efficiency* of the Community institutions, by providing the necessary programming tool that can help determine in a rational way the specific objectives to be attained in legislative business during the reference period and direct the deployment of the appropriate resources.

The bases for the programme

To reflect these needs for efficiency and transparency, the programme, which first saw the light of day as a forecasting instrument as a Commission initiative in 1988, is based on a set of objectives directly inspired by the Communities' constitutional instruments.

For 1993, the programme follows the structure of these constitutional instruments — the existing Treaties and, provisionally pending completion of the procedures for its ratification, the Treaty on European Union. Within this provisional structure, the specific status conferred by that Treaty on the common foreign and security policy (the 'second pillar') and cooperation in justice and home affairs (the 'third pillar') is highlighted.

It should be pointed out that Commission proposals for legislation are subjected to a comprehensive examination of the costs and benefits for the public authorities of the Member States and for all interested parties.

The underlying purpose of the legislative programme is to offer a comprehensive overview in a dynamic time frame of all principal legislative activity (excluding purely executive or delegated instruments). It covers measures currently in preparation at the Commission which are to be presented: proposals for directives, regulations and decisions, including those relating to international agreements.

Subsidiarity

This programme contains 100 items of new legislation to be proposed, plus 50 proposals for amendment, integration or updating of existing instruments, 19 consolidation measures and some 50 international agreements.

The Commission must emphasize that the legislative programme is purely indicative as regards both substance and timing; its intention is to comply with the principle of subsidiarity by closely examining all the draft proposals listed in it which do not fall within the areas where the Community has exclusive competence, so as to establish whether the proposed action can best be carried out at Community level. In the same spirit, having due regard for the principle of proportionality, every proposal will be carefully examined so as to confine Community management and monitoring to what is strictly necessary.

The following Annexes are attached:

   I. List of pending proposals mentioned in Annex 2 to Part A of the Conclusions of the Presidency on the December 1992 Edinburgh European Council;

  II. List of subjects on which Green or White Papers, not necessarily leading to legislation, are to be prepared in 1993;

 III. List of principal legislative proposals already made by the Commission and still pending before the other institutions.

Explanatory notes

Each item of legislation is preceded by a dash (—).

The description of each item is so drafted as to bring out its content and purpose.

The following identifiers are used:

○: forthcoming proposals which, it would appear at first sight, should be preceded by broad discussions;

○○: forthcoming proposals which at first sight require specific assessment of their impact on business in general and on small business in particular.

1.	CITIZENS' RIGHTS
2.	PROMOTING BALANCED AND SUSTAINABLE ECONOMIC AND SOCIAL PROGRESS
21.	**An area without internal frontiers**
211.	Ensuring the smooth operation of the Single Market
2111.	Free movement of goods
2112.	Free movement of persons, freedom of establishment and legal environment for business activities
2113.	Free movement of services
2114.	Free movement of capital and payments
2115.	Competition policy
2116.	Interoperability of network systems
2117.	Consumer protection
212.	Common commercial policy
213.	Common agricultural policy
214.	Common fisheries policy
215.	Common transport policy
22.	**Increasing economic and social cohesion**
221.	Structural activities
222.	Trans-European networks
223.	Overseas departments and territories
23.	**Stimulating growth and establishing an economic and monetary union**
231.	A closely coordinated economic policy
232.	Defining a single monetary policy
233.	Stimulating economic growth

24.	**Promoting sustainable, environment-friendly growth**
241.	Environment policy
242.	Research and technological development
243.	Industry and small business
244.	Energy
25.	**Promoting a high level of employment and social protection**
251.	Social policy
252.	Vocational training
26.	**Promoting a better quality of life**
261.	Consumer protection
262.	Public health
263.	Education and youth
264.	Culture
265.	Civil protection
3.	AFFIRMING THE UNION'S IDENTITY ON THE INTERNATIONAL SCENE
31.	**Establishing a common foreign and security policy** (¹)
311.	European Political Cooperation
312.	Implementing the common foreign and security policy
32.	**Enlargement**
33.	**European Economic Area and other relations with the Member States of the European Free Trade Association**
34.	**Policy on cooperation and relations with developing countries and other associated countries**
341.	Countries of central and eastern Europe and the independent States of the former Soviet Union
342.	Mediterranean, Middle East and Gulf countries
343.	Countries of Africa, the Caribbean and the Pacific
344.	Countries of Asia and Latin America
345.	Horizontal and general cooperation and aid measures
35.	**Multilateral and bilateral relations with the industrialized countries**
36.	**Relations with international organizations**
4.	DEVELOPING CLOSE COOPERATION IN THE FIELDS OF JUSTICE AND HOME AFFAIRS (²)
5.	FUNCTIONING
51.	**Financing**
52.	**European statistical system**
53.	**Programming and transparency**
531.	Consolidation of Community legislation
532.	Information for the public
54.	**Community administration**

(¹) Second pillar (Title V of the Treaty on European Union).
(²) Third pillar (Title VI of the Treaty on European Union).

PROGRAMME

Continuing the task of laying the foundations of an ever closer union among the peoples of Europe, maintaining and building on the 'acquis communautaire' on the basis of the existing Treaties, and playing a full part, once ratification of the Treaty on European Union signed at Maastricht on 7 February 1992 has been completed, in the task, assigned to the Union by that Treaty, of organizing relations between the Member States and between their peoples in an integrated and cohesive fashion, by working towards the new goal of economic and monetary union, backed up by the Single Market and structural policies, and gradually supplemented by implementation of a common foreign and security policy and by enhanced cooperation in the fields of justice and home affairs

1. CITIZENS' RIGHTS

   Once ratification of the Treaty on European Union is completed, protection of the rights and interests of Member States' nationals will have to be strengthened by gradually giving substance to Union citizenship to supplement national citizenship, which will include the right to travel and settle freely in the territory of the Member States.

   o — Right to vote and stand in elections for the European Parliament in the Member State of residence

2. PROMOTING BALANCED AND SUSTAINABLE ECONOMIC AND SOCIAL PROGRESS

   The Community must at one and the same time consolidate and balance its aims in competition, cooperation and solidarity, pursuing the top priority of boosting job creation and lowering unemployment, incorporating essential environmental requirements in the definition and implementation of its policies, reinforcing economic and social cohesion in the Community, as a fundamental pillar of political union, and of development cooperation in policies liable to affect the developing countries, improving competitiveness and taking care to ensure that any financial or administrative burden falling on the Community, national governments, local authorities, economic operators or the citizen is kept to the minimum and is proportionate to the goal to be achieved.

21. AN AREA WITHOUT INTERNAL FRONTIERS

   In the present economic environment, one of the Community's priority objectives in 1993 must be to enable individuals and firms to derive the maximum benefit from the Single Market and thus stimulate economic activity.

211. **Ensuring the smooth operation of the Single Market**

   In order to make a success of the Single Market, the Commission will rise to the challenge of managing this market and will endeavour to eliminate the remaining barriers to the exercise of the four fundamental freedoms and prevent the emergence of new ones, while leaving as much scope for decisions at national level as is compatible with attainment of the aim in question and the requirements of the Treaty.

   — Vocational training for customs officers: adaptation of the Matthaeus multiannual Community action programme to ensure the efficient functioning of the frontier-free internal area and the uniform application of Community customs legislation at its external frontiers

   — Mutual recognition of national rules: introduction of an information procedure

2111. Free movement of goods

   Veterinary matters

   oo — Livestock products and live animals: fees for veterinary inspections

   — Products imported from non-member countries: amendment to the current Directive on veterinary inspections

   — Well-being of animals during transport

Animal feedingstuffs

— Micro-organisms and enzymes in animal feedingstuffs: legal status of possibilities for their use

— Animal feedingstuffs: laying down principles for the organization of controls

Plant health and quality of plant products

o o — Plant health products: establishment of uniform principles for granting authorization to place on the market and for evaluation

Technical and legal matters

Health protection

Pharmaceutical products

— European Agency for the Evaluation of Medicinal Products: Financial Regulation

Foodstuffs

o o — Mineral and spring waters: replacing Directive 80/777/EEC by harmonization under the 'new approach', confined to essential requirements

Environmental protection

o — Biocides for non-agricultural use and their active ingredients: laying down common rules for granting national authorization to place on the market (guidelines and settlement of conflicts)

o
o o — Emissions of volatile organic compounds resulting from the storage of petrol and its distribution from terminals to service stations: stage 2

o — Biodegradability of detergents: amendment, for certain uses, of the minimum thresholds laid down by framework Directive 73/404/EEC, in order to take account of environmental developments

Safety protection

o o — Cable installations for public passenger transport: essential safety conditions

o
o o — Pressure vessels: harmonization of essential safety requirements to ensure a consistent approach

— Two- or three-wheel motor vehicles: harmonization ('old approach') of the final aspects or characteristics to complete the EEC type-approval procedure introduced by framework Directive 92/61/EEC

— Motor vehicles other than private cars: harmonization ('old approach') of interior fittings in buses and coaches as regards inflammability, supplementing framework Directive 92/53/EEC

— Aerosols for decorative and recreational use: amendment of Directive 76/769/EEC to limit the use of inflammable gases

o o — Asbestos: restrictions on placing on the market for certain uses

— Gas appliances: extending the scope of Directive 90/396/EEC to appliances using fuels other than gas to ensure a consistent approach to safety

— Adapting to technical progress existing harmonization legislation ('old approach') on certain components of motor vehicles, motor cars, and agricultural and forestry tractors

Fair trading

○○ — Articles made of precious metals (gold, silver, platinum, palladium): harmonization of essential requirements

○○ — *In vitro* diagnosis: harmonization of rules in line with the outcome of work by the European Standardization Committee

Taxation

— Special VAT scheme for automobiles: common rules defining new cars

— Registration and road taxes for automobiles: common rules on temporary use

— Excise duty on mineral oils: introduction of rules on the colouring and marking of oils used, at reduced rates, as car fuel

— Tobacco and alcoholic beverages: gradual raising of the tax-free allowances laid down by Directive 92/12/EEC

○
○○ — Annual taxes on private motor vehicles: harmonization of structure by establishing a consistent and fair base in the light of environmental problems and harmful emissions

— Tax allowances for losses inherent in the nature of dutiable products in the course of production, processing and storage: conditions for granting such allowances

— Rates of duty: adjustment of the target rates laid down in Directive 92/12/EEC, in line with developments

2112. Free movement of persons, freedom of establishment and legal environment for business activities

Ensuring freedom of establishment and freedom of residence for Community citizens, creating a propitious legal environment for businesses.

Facilitating access to self-employed activities and their performance and encouraging mutual recognition of diplomas, certificates and qualifications

○ — Collectively regulated occupations: establishment of Community rules for cross-border activities so as to remove obstacles caused by differences between national regulations

○ — Legal professions: preparation of a proposal for a directive to improve the rules on right of establishment currently applying to the professions

Company law and company taxation

○○ — Cross-border cooperation between companies of different Member States: extension of scope of Directives 90/434/EEC (Mergers) and 90/435/EEC (Parent companies/subsidiaries) to cover all forms of company subject to corporation tax

○
○○ — Annual and consolidated accounts: amendment of Fourth and Seventh Directives 78/660/EEC and 83/349/EEC to extend their scope to financial conglomerates

○○ — European company: taxation arrangements applicable to transfers of places of business

Intellectual and industrial property

— Plant health products: introduction of a supplementary protection certificate

○
○○ — Industrial designs and models: legal protection rules, creation of a Community Industrial Designs and Models Office and coordination of the national rules relating to the term of protection and the legal effect

32   S. 1/93

2113. Free movement of services

Ensuring the freedom to offer services in the case of operators established in a Member State other than that of the recipient of the service so as to encourage competition, increase competitiveness and extend the range of choice offered to private users and to businesses within the single market.

Telecommunications services

In the light of the conclusions to be drawn from the consultations on the Green Paper on postal services published in July 1992 and the report on the situation of telecommunications services submitted in October 1992, the Commission will deliberate on guidelines for the substantive and scheduling aspects of any subsequent legislative proposals required to ensure the proper operation of the common market.

New technologies and information technologies

Standardization

o — Provision of satellite telecommunications services: approximation of the laws of the Member States on the mutual recognition of licences

Transport services

— Hiring of heavy goods vehicles and buses in other Member States: removal of certain restrictions

Financial services

— Coordination of certain undertakings for collective investment in transferable securities (Ucits): extension of the scope of Directive 85/611/EEC to such undertakings which invest their assets in money market instruments and to those which invest their assets in shares issued by other such undertakings, to make them subject to a single approval system

— Supervision of credit institutions: measures to strengthen and clarify the role of auditors in the light of the analysis of the implications of the BCCI affair

— possibility for supervisory authority to refuse or cancel authorization when the structure of a group becomes opaque

— correspondence in one country between real place of business and registered office

— strengthening of intra-Community cooperation between regulatory authorities and other bodies

— obligation for auditors to report to supervisory authorities any facts casting doubt on the solvency of the institution

o — Prudential supervision of financial groups (credit, insurance, stock exchange institutions): measures to supplement the Directive in force relating to supervision on a consolidated basis (92/30/EEC) in order to establish the conditions for adequate supervision

— System for indemnifying investors in transferable securities: minimum protection against bankruptcy, winding-up, fraud, etc. of the issuing companies

Audiovisual services

Regulatory aspects

o — Copyright and neighbouring rights: harmonization of the rules applicable to the private copying of
oo sound and audiovisual works

Technological aspects

— High definition television (HDTV): harmonization of the different means of broadcasting (satellite, cable, land-based) and of the different technologies possible (analog or digital) in order to ensure the interoperability of the new HDTV systems

Audiovisual production

— Media programme of measures to promote the development of the audiovisual industry: evaluation and amendment of Decision 90/685/EEC which established the programme

2114. Free movement of capital and payments

Ensuring that there are no restrictions on the movement of capital and payments between Member States of the Community and, in due course, between Member States and non-member countries.

2115. Competition policy

Creating a level playing field by taking action against agreements, concerted practices, abuse of dominant positions and mergers which are incompatible with the common market, government subsidies, exclusive rights and dumping.

o — Merger control: revision of certain provisions of Regulation (EEC) No 4064/89

2116. Interoperability of network systems

Contributing to the functioning of the internal market and enabling citizens of the union, economic operators and local and regional authorities to derive full benefit from the setting up of an area without internal frontiers.

Ensuring the interoperability of networks, in particular by harmonization of technical standards

- Data-transmission connections between Community and national departments: programme for the development of interchange of data between administrations (IDA) networks

oo — Intra-Community trade statistics: establishment of a computerized data-transmission infrastructure for collection, processing and distribution

- Satellite telecommunications: approximation of national laws with a view to improving access to telecommunications space segments in Europe

- High-speed train network: rules to ensure technical interoperability of networks

- Security of information systems: approximation of national laws by extending the current plan of action, adopted by the Council on 31 March 1992

2117. Consumer protection

Contributing to the attainment of a high level of consumer protection through measures concerned with the establishment and functioning of the internal market.

o — Information concerning certain foodstuffs: harmonization of national legislation to increase trans-
oo   parency (to complement Directives 79/112/EEC, 84/450/EEC and 90/496/EEC)

212. **Common commercial policy**

Safeguarding the unity of the Single Market through implementation of uniform common import arrangements, contributing to the harmonious development of world trade through liberalization, while maintaining appropriate trade protection.

- National tariff quotas: total elimination

- Anti-counterfeiting measures: introduction of uniform rules to protect the Community's economy and reassure consumers and manufacturers

- *European pharmacopoeia:* signing by the Community of the Council of Europe Convention, harmonization of human medicine tests, harmonization of veterinary medicines

- Duty-free allowance for travellers: re-drafting of the Regulation ((EEC) No 918/83) currently in force in accordance with a concept which takes account of the fiscal aspects of the question, so as to ensure uniform implementation of Community law

- Imports of ECSC products originating in GATT countries, countries accorded like treatment and non-GATT (primarily State-trading) countries: introduction of Community arrangements

213. **Common agricultural policy**

As part of the changing agricultural policy, achieving rational development of agricultural production in the Community, technical progress and optimum utilization of production factors, particularly labour, while ensuring a fair standard of living for the agricultural community, market stability, security of supply and reasonable prices for consumers.

Implementing the reforms adopted in 1992 with a view to bringing about more balanced markets, improving both the internal and international competitiveness of the Community's agricultural sector, providing farmers with more stable incomes and ensuring that the Community's resources are distributed more fairly, while maintaining the social and economic balance in rural areas, in particular by environmental protection and, at the same time, observing the basic principles of the common agricultural policy (unity of the market, Community preference and financial solidarity).

— Sugar: common market organization

— Wine: reform of the common market organization

— Alcohol of agricultural origin: establishment of a common market organization replacing the various national arrangements, designed to remove all obstacles to free movement, superseding the proposal pending since 1981

— Accompanying measures for the reform of the common agricultural policy, adopted in 1992 (early retirement, afforestation, environmental protection measures, including extensification and set-aside of land)

o — Community genetic heritage and bio-diversity: coordination of Member States' efforts concerning the conservation, characterization and use of genetic resources in agriculture

— Agricultural prices and related measures for 1993/94

214. **Common fisheries policy**

Sustaining fishery resources by rationalizing fishing activities and ensuring the economic and social viability of the industry in the Community by regulating access to external resources and developing control mechanisms and sources of supply.

— Regulation of fishing operations in the area of the North-West Atlantic Fisheries Organization

— Act of Accession of Spain and Portugal to the European Communities: amendment of certain accession arrangements regarding fisheries in the light of the discussions on the 1992 report

— Fishing activities using static gear: amendment of technical measures for the conservation of fishery resources (Regulation (EEC) No 3094/86)

— Limits on fishing: setting of total allowable catches and quotas, and related measures for 1994

— Prices of fishery products for 1994

— Access of waters of non-member countries for Community fishing vessels: negotiation or renegotiation of new fishing agreements with the Russian Federation, Canada, Seychelles, São Tomé, Guinea-Bissau, Gambia, Mauritania, Mozambique, Mauritius, Guinea, Gabon, India, Namibia, Chile, Colombia, Ecuador, Mexico, Peru, Uruguay and Venezuela

215. **Common transport policy**

Reinforcing and completing the operation of the Single Market, through the establishment of a genuine common transport market by ensuring lasting mobility, improving safety standards, providing better living and working conditions for transport workers, developing and integrating transport systems in the Community and building up outside links.

In the light of the discussions on the White Paper on the development of the transport policy published in December 1992 the Commission has finalized its guidelines.

Economic measures and regulations

- Rail transport: drawing-up of common rules on establishment of companies, allocation of infrastructure capacity and charges for the use of railway infrastructure

oo — Carriage of goods by inland waterway: adjustment of 'tour de rôle' system and other positive measures

oo — Fees for intra-Community air services: introduction of principles and criteria for setting fees

Harmonization measures

- Weights and dimensions of road vehicles: application of Directive 85/3/EEC to national traffic

- Tachograph: alterations to incorporate technological developments and amendment of Regulation (EEC) No 3821/85

Transport safety

- Establishment of database on road accidents (CARE)

- Carriage of dangerous goods: Community standards for the application to national traffic of international arrangements (ADR/RID) and uniform procedures

- Carriage by sea of dangerous and polluting goods: minimum requirements for ships entering or leaving Community seaports, designed to ensure that the authorities are properly informed and can take appropriate action should there be an incident (Phase II)

- Control of ships by the port State: tighter measures

- International rules and certain resolutions of the Intrnational Maritime Organization: convergent application in the Community

- Introduction of common safety rules for:

o — marine equipment

— training for seamen

- Introduction of common rules and standards for classification societies and technical shipbuilding standards

Transport ecology

o — 'NO$_x$' emissions from new aircraft: reduction in two stages not affecting engines currently in production

External matters

- Inland waterway transport: requirements for entry into the Community for vessels from non-member countries

- Civil aviation: negotiation of agreements with Switzerland and certain countries in central and eastern Europe

22. INCREASING ECONOMIC AND SOCIAL COHESION

Promoting harmonious development of the Community as a whole, in partnership with Member States, firms and regions, by narrowing the regional development gap; helping less-favoured regions, including rural areas and outermost regions to catch up; making the employment of workers easier, increasing their geographic and occupational mobility, and facilitating their adaptation to industrial change and changes in production systems.

221. Structural activities

In the light of the conclusions reached by the Edinburgh European Council, the Commission will propose the necessary measures to adjust the structural policies. It has already proposed a temporary legal basis for early establishment of the Cohesion Fund and a definitive regulation

— Reform for the Structural Funds: revision of the basic Regulations ((EEC) No 2052/88 and (EEC) No 4253/88)

— European Regional Development Fund: amendment of Regulation (EEC) No 4254/88

— European Social Fund: amendment of Regulation (EEC) No 4255/88 to render the employment of workers easier, to increase their geographic and occupational mobility and to facilitate their adaptation to industrial change and changes in production systems in particular through vocational training and retraining

— EAGGF (Guidance Section): amendment of Regulation (EEC) No 4256/88

— EAGGF (Guidance Section): adaptation of Regulations (EEC) No 2328/91, (EEC) No 866/90 and (EEC) No 867/90 on improving the efficiency of agricultural structures and the conditions for the processing and marketing of agricultural and forestry products

— Inclusion of the structural components of the common fisheries policy in the revision of the Structural Funds Regulations

222. Trans-European networks

Contributing, notably through support programmes, to economic and social cohesion by encouraging the interconnection and interoperability of national networks and access to these networks; promoting the establishment and development of trans-European networks, and taking account of the need to provide links between island, enclave and remote regions and central regions of the Community.

Defining and implementing guidelines on objectives, priorities and main lines of action

— Master plans for traditional railways, ports, airports, management of air traffic and shipping

Telecommunications

— Integrated services digital network (ISDN): objectives and priorities for the coordination of action by the Member States to ensure interoperability

— Broadband services network: objectives and priorities for the coordination of action by the Member States to ensure interoperability (pilot phase)

Energy

— Natural gas and electricity networks: identification of missing links and projects of common interest

23. STIMULATING GROWTH AND ESTABLISHING ECONOMIC AND MONETARY UNION

Regenerating economic momentum by implementing the European growth initiative, strengthening competitiveness and making progress towards establishing EMU

231. **A closely coordinated economic policy**

Improving economic policy coordination and the convergence of economic performance

— Economic convergence: annual report for 1993 on the economic situation in the Community

— Economic convergence: annual report for 1994 on the economic situation in the Community

— Preparations for Stage II of economic and monetary union:

— detailed rules for prohibiting privileged access by the public sector to financial institutions

— rules for applying the ban on monetary financing of public deficits

232. **Defining a single monetary policy**

Preparing for a single monetary and exchange rate policy with a view to the irrevocable fixing of exchange rates as a preliminary to the introduction of a single currency, the ecu, and the maintenance of price stability.

— Preparations for Stage II of economic and monetary union:

— rules on compilation of the statistics to be used to determine the key for capital subscriptions to the European Monetary Institute

— setting the limits and conditions for consultation of the European Monetary Institute by Member States on proposed legislation in areas falling within its competence

233. **Stimulating economic growth**

The Edinburgh European Council agreed on an action programme to stimulate economic growth in Europe. This programme contains a number of initiatives by Member States and Community authorities. The Community measures come under various chapters of the legislative programme: the area without internal frontiers, cohesion, research, trans-European networks, etc.

24. PROMOTING SUSTAINABLE, ENVIRONMENT-FRIENDLY GROWTH

241. **Environment policy**

Aiming for a high level of protection, with allowance for regional diversity; applying the principle of preventive action, the principle of correction, preferably at source, of attacks on the environment and the 'polluter pays' principle; implementing the fifth Community action programme against a background of radical change in current forms of growth, production, consumption, and behaviour patterns within the Community and practice at global, regional, national, local and, indeed, personal level.

o — Integrated pollution control: introduction of an integrated system to limit and prevent emissions which
oo pollute air, water and soil

— Environmental impact assessment: revision and/or extension of existing instruments

Contributing to conservation, protection and improvement of the quality of the environment

Air

○ — Consumption of HCFCs: control in the Community following the November 1992 revision of the Montreal Protocol with a view to phasing-out substances that deplete the ozone layer

○ — Products containing CFCs or halons originating in countries not party to the Montreal Protocol: ban on imports into the Community

— Monitoring and evaluation of air quality: introduction of framework standards to harmonize monitoring rules to promote the comparability of data and harmonize health protection criteria

— Basic air quality data: improvement of comparability and transparency to secure a coherent overview of the impact of measures to reduce emissions

— Revision of the 'Seveso' Directive

Water

○ — Ecological quality of surface waters: introduction of procedures for the gradual improvement of the aquatic environment in line with objectives set by Member States

○ — Protection of bathing waters: adaptation of Directive 76/150/EEC to clarify its provisions and take account of new scientific knowledge

○ — Quality of drinking water: amendment of Directive 80/778/EEC to adapt it to scientific progress and extend it to all water for domestic use

Developing international cooperation (follow-up to the June 1992 Rio Summit)

— Montreal Protocol: revision

242. **Research and technological development (R&TD)**

In partnership with the Member States, industry, research centres and universities, promoting high-quality R&TD in order to increase the international competitiveness of Community industry and to improve the quality of life by increasing the selectivity, quality and effectiveness of the research effort, by encouraging cooperation and promoting coherence between national policies, by enabling the potential of the internal market to be exploited in full throughout the Community, by increasing cooperation with non-member countries and international organizations, by promoting the dissemination and utilization of R&TD results, by stimulating the training and mobility of researchers and by promoting the coordination of national R&TD policies.

— Fourth framework programme of research and technological development (1994 to 1998): programme consolidating and concentrating the full range of R&TD and industrial innovation activities with a view to maintaining the competitiveness of European industry and using science and technology to serve society

○ — Fourth framework programme of research and technological development (1994 to 1998): establishing rules for the participation of industry, research centres and universities and for the dissemination of research results

— Fourth framework programme of research and technological development (1994 to 1998): first specific R&TD programmes

Developing international scientific and technical cooperation

— EEC-Canada: negotiation of an agreement on scientific and technical cooperation

243. **Industry and small business**

Enhancing the competitiveness of firms in a system of open and competitive markets, supported by the establishment of trans-European networks, backed by the research effort and anticipating change.

Coal and steel industries

On the general assumption that the Treaty establishing the European Coal and Steel Community will duly expire in July 2002, making use of the flexibility of the Treaty to adapt its application to the situation in the coal and steel industries and organizing their gradual incorporation into the EEC Treaty, focusing on the financial instruments and social provisions.

244. **Energy**

Improving the Community's energy balance

Promoting the development and dissemination of energy technologies

○ — Demonstration of innovating technology and dissemination and utilization of the results of techno-
○○ logical development: Community support to enhance security of supply, to improve the quality of the environment and to promote the rational use of resources both as part of the follow-up to the Community Thermie programme and under the fourth framework programme of research and technological development (1994 to 1998)

Promoting energy efficiency and new and renewable energy sources

— Efficiency of domestic appliances: introduction of standards designed to achieve a 10 to 15 % improvement over a four-year period and a corresponding reduction in CO_2 emissions and to remove obstacles to intra-Community trade

External aspects

— European Energy Charter: negotiation and conclusion of a basic agreement setting out general rules on trade in energy, conditions for investment and environmental protection, and of sectoral protocols on cooperation (nuclear safety, energy efficiency, oil and gas) with the G-24 countries, the countries of Central and Eastern Europe and the independent States of the former Soviet Union

— Community accession to the International Energy Agency: amendment of the pending recommendation for negotiating directives

25. PROMOTING A HIGH LEVEL OF EMPLOYMENT AND SOCIAL PROTECTION

Developing the social dimension of the internal market and consolidating Community cohesion and competitiveness by strengthening social policy, with due regard for the diversity of national systems, cultures and practices, and by developing vocational training.

251. **Social policy**

Promoting employment, improving living and working conditions, providing proper social protection, promoting and developing the dialogue between management and labour at European level with a view to arriving at relations based on agreement, developing human resources with a view to sustainable high employment, and combating social exclusion.

Improving health protection and safety at the workplace by harmonizing conditions while maintaining the improvements made and by the gradual application of minimum rules (through individual directives within the meaning of framework Directive 89/391/EEC).

— Protection of workers against risks related to exposure to chemical agents: minimum requirements implementing Community rules and regulations on chemical agents and measures in force for the protection of the outside environment

○○ — Specific work equipment: minimum health and safety requirements relating to rules for the use and periodic inspection of equipment, supplementing Directive 89/655/EEC and directives in force on freedom of movement

Providing protection for employees in the event of termination of contract

○○ — Safeguarding employees' rights in the event of transfers of undertakings: amendment of Directive 77/187/EEC on the approximation of legislation

Combating social exclusion and encouraging the integration of persons excluded from the labour market.

— Combating social exclusion: support, innovation and exchange programme to promote exchanges of experience and consciousness-raising among the parties concerned

252. **Vocational training**

By means of encouragement, cooperation and support between Member States, helping to develop quality training, to set up a European area of qualifications and to promote growth-stimulating initiatives, in particular by catering for industrial change.

○ — Vocational qualifications: introduction of a system of transparency based on cooperation between
○○ Member States

Improving initial and continuing training

— Force programme for the development of continuing vocational training in the Community: reorganization, rationalization and extension of current Community measures (Eurotecnet programme and Iris network)

Facilitating access to vocational training and encouraging mobility of instructors and trainees, particularly young people

— Petra programme for training and preparation of young people for adult and working life (1987 to 1994): modifications designed to consolidate application and to increase participation by the two sides of industry

Stimulating cooperation on training between educational or training establishments and firms

— Comett programme to encourage cooperation between higher education and industry in the field of technology — Phase III: launching of Comett III

Fostering cooperation with third countries and the competent international organizations in the sphere of vocational training

— European Training Foundation: updating of draft regulation establishing the Foundation to take account of the vocational training requirements of the Commonwealth of Independent States

— European Training Foundation: conditions of employment for staff

— Cooperation between the Community and the USA: launching of a Community scheme in the field of vocational training and higher education

Developing exchange of information and experience on issues common to the training systems of the Member States

○ — Trans-European networks in the field of vocational training and education: support for action by the Member States

26. PROMOTING A BETTER QUALITY OF LIFE

Strengthening solidarity between the peoples of Europe with due regard for their individuality, history, culture and traditions.

261. **Consumer production**

Supporting and complementing Member States' policies to achieve a high level of protection for the health and physical safety and the economic and legal interests of consumers and to provide them with appropriate information.

262. **Public health**

Contributing to a high level of health protection, by promoting cooperation between Member States, supporting and complementing their efforts where necessary but stopping short of harmonization.

Promoting cooperation with non-member countries and international organizations

— EEC-Asean: negotiation and conclusion of an agreement to strengthen international action to prevent the deflection of precursors for the illicit manufacture of narcotic drugs and psychotropic substances

263. **Education and youth**

Contributing to the development of quality education provision, by promoting cooperation between the Member States and the involvement of young people in European integration, supporting and complementing the measures taken by the Member States.

Developing the European dimension of education by promoting the study and dissemination of the languages of the Member States

— Lingua programme for the promotion of language skills (1990 to 1994): extension by one year to attain the objectives of the programme and to take account of the requirements of the various sectors of economic life

Facilitating student and teacher mobility by promoting academic recognition of diplomas and periods of study

o — Erasmus student mobility programme (third phase): launching of Erasmus III to follow up the 1987 to 1993 programme with the aim of increasing student mobility, promoting inter-university cooperation, encouraging teacher mobility and creating a pool of graduates with direct experience in intra-Comunity cooperation

Developing the exchange of information and experience on problems common to the education systems of the Member States

— Education in the Community and the European Economic Area: creation of an information network based on the Eurydice experience to promote exchange of information on national education systems

Facilitating the development of exchanges of young people and youth workers

— Youth for Europe programme 1992 to 1994 (third phase): rationalization of existing actions to complement policy and action at national level

264. **Culture**

Contributing to the flowering of the cultures of the Member States, while respecting national diversity and bringing the common cultural heritage to the fore, by encouraging cooperation between the Member States, complementing and supporting their efforts where necessary but stopping short of harmonization.

The audiovisual sector is covered in section 2113.

3. **AFFIRMING THE UNION'S IDENTITY ON THE INTERNATIONAL SCENE**

Strengthening new international responsibilities in the new architecture of Europe in order to contribute to the future equilibrium of the continent and to the harmonious development of international relations, while ensuring that the Community's external activities are based on and backed up by strong and stable common internal policies.

31. ESTABLISHING A COMMON FOREIGN AND SECURITY POLICY

Affirming the European identity on the international scene once the Treaty on European Union has been ratified, by putting a common foreign and security policy into effect, eventually leading to the framing of a common defence policy which might in time lead to a common defence, with the objective of safeguarding common values, fundamental interests and independence, strengthening security, preserving international security, and developing and consolidating democracy and the rule of law and respect for human rights and fundamental freedoms.

311. **European Political Cooperation**

In the exercise of its own powers, the Commission will seek to achieve and to maintain coherence between the various policies of the Member States and to promote European political cooperation

— Regional economic cooperation in the Middle East: implementation of the guidelines emerging from political cooperation in the light of progress in the peace process

312. **Implementing the common foreign and security policy**

Once ratification of the Treaty on European Union is completed, the Commission will exercise its right of initiative to gradually implement common action in those areas where the Member States have substantial interests in common while seeking to ensure coherence between external action, economic policy and development policy.

32. ENLARGEMENT

Progress along the lines laid down by the Treaty on European Union, with proper regard for the essential components of the European identity, the democratic system, respect for human rights and the capacity of the applicant countries to accept and apply the *acquis communautaire* and the common foreign and security policy.

— Accession of Austria, Sweden and Finland: negotiations

— Accession of Norway: presentation of the Commission's opinion

— Accession of Malta: presentation of the Commission's opinion

— Accession of Cyprus: presentation of the Commission's opinion

33. EUROPEAN ECONOMIC AREA AND OTHER RELATIONS WITH THE MEMBER STATES OF THE EUROPEAN FREE TRADE ASSOCIATION

Progress towards implementation of the Agreement signed at Oporto on 2 May 1992, establishing a European Economic Area between the Community and the Member States of the European Free Trade Association as an integrated, dynamic and homogeneous economic entity founded on common rules relating to the four freedoms, rules of fair competition and shared policies, in the general context of relations based on proximity, shared values regarding democracy and the market economy and a common European identity.

— European Economic Area: implementation of planned tariff measures

34. POLICY ON COOPERATION AND RELATIONS WITH DEVELOPING COUNTRIES AND OTHER ASSOCIATED COUNTRIES

Promoting cooperation for the development of non-member countries or groups of such countries or giving them associations with the Community, either multilaterally or bilaterally, with a view to developing and consolidating democracy, the rule of law and respect for human rights and fundamental freedoms in non-member countries and thereby encouraging the sustainable economic and social development of the developing countries, especially the least-developed of them, and the fight against poverty there and harmoniously and progressively integrating them into the world economy, and boosting the support given to the economic and political reform processes launched in the countries of central and eastern Europe and in the members of the CIS.

— Framework for Community medium and long-term macroeconomic and financial assistance to non-member countries

341. **Countries of central and eastern Europe and the independent States of the former Soviet Union**

With support from the Tacis technical assistance programmes, advancing towards closer links and broader cooperation with the independent States of the former Soviet Union so as to generate the conditions required for establishment of a market economy and a democratic society; with support from the Phare programme of multilateral cooperation and assistance and the food aid programmes, advancing towards closer association with the countries of central and eastern Europe, by developing the bilateral relations established by the current or future Europe Agreements with Poland, Hungary, the Czech and Slovak Republics, Romania and Bulgaria so as to bring these countries into the process of European integration with a prospect of ultimate accession, and developing the relations established by the trade and cooperation agreements with Albania and the Baltic States

— EEC-independent States of the former Soviet Union/Baltic States/Mongolia/former Yugoslavia/Albania/Romania/Bulgaria: negotiation of bilateral textile agreements

— Contracting parties to the Common Transit Convention (EEC/Member States of the European Free Trade Association) — Hungary/Poland/Czech and Slovak Republics: establishment of relations concerning transit procedures with a view to helping these countries adopt modern customs legislation and confirm their transition to a market economy

— EEC-Bulgaria/Romania/Slovenia: tariff measures provided for in the Europe Agreements to come into effect

— European Investment Bank loans in countries of central and eastern Europe: renewal of all Community guarantees

342. **Mediterranean, Middle East and Gulf countries**

Working for a comprehensive strategy which, looking beyond the restoration of peace and the pursuit of humanitarian aid, consists of establishing Treaty-based relations with the States of former Yugoslavia, promoting the implementation of the reformed Mediterranean policy elaborated in 1992 for the harmonious development of the peoples of the southern countries of the basin through the fourth bilateral financial protocols, for that purpose accelerating the dismantling of tariff barriers and boosting support for regional projects, and launching a new form of partnership-based cooperation with the Maghreb countries.

— Textiles: negotiation of an extension of the preferential arrangements with Turkey, Morocco, Tunisia, Egypt, Malta

— EEC-Israel: negotiation of an extension to the scope of the free trade agreement in force since 1975, in the context of regional economic cooperation in the Middle East

— EEC-Tunisia: negotiation and conclusion of a Europe-Maghreb type agreement on a partnership basis

— EEC-Cyprus: negotiation of a cooperation agreement to allow audiovisual professionals in Cyprus to take part in the Media programme

— Reformed Mediterranean policy: negotiation of improvements to the protocols on rules of origin

343. **Countries of Africa, the Caribbean and the Pacific**

Full implementation of the Fourth Lomé Convention for the association between the Community and the 69 ACP countries under national and regional framework programmes, including support for structural adjustment, and preparing for the mid-term review.

344. **Countries of Asia and Latin America**

Implementing financial and technical cooperation in accordance with the new multiannual guidelines that came into force in 1992, while broadening cooperation with the Asian countries and pursuing the process of strengthening bilateral and multilateral relations with Latin America, notably through third-generation bilateral agreements extending to industrial cooperation, the development of human resources and environmental protection.

— EEC-Vietnam: negotiation and conclusion of an economic cooperation agreement

345. **Horizontal and general cooperation and aid measures**

Humanitarian aid

○○ — Food aid and emergency food aid: amendment of the current Regulation (EEC) No 3972/86 applicable to the developing countries to extend it to all non-member countries and of the Regulations on general rules for the mobilization of food aid ((EEC) No 2200/87) and detailed rules for the application of the basic Regulation ((EEC) No 1420/87)

Horizontal cooperation measures

— Tropical forests: definition, in the context of implementation of the conclusions of the June 1992 Rio de Janeiro Conference, of the objectives and means of Community action for the sustainable conservation and management of resources

General cooperation measures

— Generalized system of preferences: review of the system and improvements to the rules of origin

— International Tropical Timber Agreement: negotiation of a new Agreement

35. MULTILATERAL AND BILATERAL RELATIONS WITH THE INDUSTRIALIZED COUNTRIES

Cooperating with Western partners in the context of a new style of partnership with the rest of the world based on the gradual entrenchment of shared values and respect for each other's interests while contributing, through the Customs Union, to the harmonious development of world trade and to the liberalization of international trade and pursuing both the closer dialogue with the United States and Canada under the Transatlantic Declarations of 1990 and 1991 and, under the Joint Declaration of July 1991, the attempts with Japan to open its market more fully to external trade and investment in the context of a coherent and comprehensive strategy.

— Uruguay Round: conclusion and implementation of the multilateral negotiations

— Customs cooperation: negotiation of a convention on a simplified scheme of international customs transit for goods carried by rail

— Customs cooperation: conclusion of the UN Convention on the temporary importation of private and commercial road vehicles

— Customs cooperation: negotiation of agreements with the United States and Canada to streamline cooperation between customs authorities and put Community operators on an equal footing in partner countries

— Textiles: upon conclusion of the Uruguay Round, integration of the industry in the GATT rules by implementation of the first stage of the Textiles protocol

— Customs cooperation: conclusion of the UN Convention on the customs treatment of containers used in international transport

36. RELATIONS WITH INTERNATIONAL ORGANIZATIONS

Ensuring proper relations or concluding agreements with international organizations to establish associations involving mutual rights and obligations, joint action and special procedures, notably in the form of close cooperation with the Organization for Economic Cooperation and Development, while maintaining all appropriate links with UN organs and specialized agencies and with the General Agreement on Tariffs and Trade and developing all appropriate forms of cooperation with the Council of Europe

4. DEVELOPING CLOSE COOPERATION IN THE FIELDS OF JUSTICE AND HOME AFFAIRS

Once ratification of the Treaty on European Union has been completed, the Commission will implement the Community measures called for by Article 100c. It will be fully associated with work on the matters listed in Article K.1, notably those where the Treaty on European Union gives it the right to share the power of initiative, for example in relation to immigration and asylum.

5. **FUNCTIONING**

Increasing democracy in the functioning of the institutions and improving efficiency and management.

51. FINANCING

Guaranteeing sufficient funds for the Community, while respecting budgetary discipline and the financial perspective.

New medium-term financial framework to accompany the second stage of Economic and Monetary Union, reflecting the Community's expanded powers under European Union.

— Revision of the own resources Decision

— General budget for 1994: preliminary draft

— ECSC budget for 1994: examination by Parliament of the Commission's draft

Financial regulations

— Financial Regulation applicable to the general budget of the Communities: updating and revision to reflect the implications of the changes brought about by the Treaty on European Union

— System of own resources: updating of Regulation (EEC) No 1552/89 implementing Decision 88/376/EEC, Euratom to take account of the reserves entered in the budget as a result of the European Council's conclusions concerning the Delors II package of structural and financial measures, including measures to combat fraud

— Financial Regulation: additions to proposal COM(92) 358 final amending the Financial Regulation of 21 December 1977 in order to take account of the reserve for humanitarian aid and the reserve for endowing the Guarantee Fund relating to borrowing and lending operations

Measures to combat fraud

— Criminal law protection of the Community's financial interests

— Irregularities involving the Structural Funds: harmonization of the statements presented by the Member States pursuant to Article 23 of Regulation (EEC) No 4253/88

52. EUROPEAN STATISTICAL SYSTEM

Establishing a Community statistical area by introducing a set of standards, methods and organizational structures capable of producing comparable, reliable and relevant statistics throughout the Community, providing the institutions and the Member States with the information they need to implement, monitor and evaluate Community policies and distributing essential statistics to all concerned with economic and social matters.

oo — Rules and principles for the production of statistics in all the Member States: coordination in order to obtain comparable data responding to the same rules and principles of organization as Community statistics

Transport

oo — Sea, road and other modes of transport: establishment of freight and passenger statistics

Business

oo — Trade: introduction of a system for the collection of structural and economic data based on harmonized and synchronized concepts capable of producing comparable results in order to back up and promote business policy and, in particular, with the aim of not making administrative obligations any more cumbersome

oo — Industry: adoption of a common method to obtain coordinated statistics on structure and activities through the annual business survey

53. PROGRAMMING AND TRANSPARENCY

531. **Consolidation of Community legislation**

Continuation of efforts to make Community rules more accessible and more concise to help individuals and businessmen find their way through the maze of legislation, by means of declaratory consolidation for information purposes (amalgamation of all amendments to original instruments) prepared by the *Publications Office of the European Communities* and by means of legislative consolidation (adoption of new legal instruments).

Legislative consolidation

Consolidating existing legislation, including amendments and adjustments delegated to the Commission, by the adoption of new official legal instruments in accordance with the normal decision-making procedure and publication in the 'L' series of the *Official Journal of the European Communities,* employing an accelerated and mutually acceptable working method to be agreed with the Council and Parliament, depending on how much of the legislation in force can be considered stable and provided that sufficient resources are available.

- Dangerous substances: classification, packaging and labelling in order to protect workers and the environment (Directive 67/548/EEC)

- Roadworthiness tests for vehicles (Directive 77/143/EEC)

- Weights, dimensions and characteristics of road vehicles (Directive 85/3/EEC)

- Admission to the occupation of road haulage operator and mutual recognition of diplomas (Directive 74/561/EEC and 77/796/EEC)

- Cosmetic products (Directive 76/768/EEC): new amendments to the proposal for consolidation which is pending (amended 20 times)

- Textile names (Directive 71/307/EEC amended three times)

- Binary textile fibre mixtures: methods for quantitative analysis (Directive 72/276/EEC amended three times)

- Excise duties on tobacco products (Directive 72/464/EEC)

- Social security (Regulations (EEC) No 1408/71 and (EEC) No 574/72)

- Oils and fats: common organization of the market (Regulation 136/66/EEC amended 24 times)

- Beef and veal: common organization of the market (Regulation (EEC) No 805/68 amended 13 times)

- Bovine animals and swine: animal health (Directive 64/432/EEC amended 24 times)

- Beet seed (Directive 66/400/EEC amended 18 times)

- Fodder plant seed (Directive 66/401/EEC amended 19 times)

- Cereal seed (Directive 66/402/EEC amended 23 times)

- Seed potatoes (Directive 66/403/EEC amended 24 times)

- Oil and fibre plants (Directive 69/208/EEC amended 24 times)

- Common catalogue of varieties (Directive 70/457/EEC amended 17 times)

- Vegetable seed (Directive 70/458/EEC amended 22 times)

54. COMMUNITY ADMINISTRATION

- Introduction of the option of payment of Community officials' salaries in ecus and introduction of the payment of their mission expenses in ecus, as part of the measures to strengthen the role of the ecu and to promote recovery and development of the ecu market

ANNEX I

LIST OF PENDING PROPOSALS TO BE REVIEWED OR WITHDRAWN, AFTER CONSULTATION OF PARLIAMENT, IN ACCORDANCE WITH THE CONCLUSIONS OF THE EDINBURGH EUROPEAN COUNCIL (ANNEX 2 TO PART A)

— Oil crisis mechanisms: review of whether to withdraw the pending proposal designed to adapt the arrangements introduced by Council Decision 77/238/EEC

— Keeping of animals in zoos: review of whether to alter the pending proposal

— Digital short-range radio-communications (DSRR): review of whether to withdraw the pending proposal on radio frequencies

— Indirect taxes on operations in securities: review of whether to withdraw the pending proposal

— Indirect taxes on the raising of capital: review of whether to withdraw the pending proposal

— Sixth VAT Directive: review of whether to withdraw the proposal for amendment currently pending

— Increase in the tax-free allowance for fuel contained in the tanks of commercial vehicles: review of whether to withdraw the pending proposal

— Temporary import arrangements for certain means of transport: review of whether to withdraw the pending proposal

— Classification of documents of Community institutions: review of whether to withdraw the pending proposal

— Network of information centres on agricultural markets and quality standards: review of whether to withdraw the pending proposal

— Public takeover bids: revision of the pending proposal relating to the thirteenth Directive on the coordination of the rules for the elimination of existing legal obstacles

— Common definition of concept of Community shipowner: revision of pending proposal

— Comparative advertising: revision of the pending proposal for a nucleus of general rules regardless of the means of communication used

— Labelling of footwear: revision of the pending proposal

— Liability of service-providers: revision of the pending proposal on coordination of national rules

— Protection of personal and private data: revision of the pending proposal concerning the approximation of the laws of the Member States with regard to mobile and fixed digital telecommunications networks

— Jams and preserves, natural mineral waters, honey, coffee extracts, fruit juices (cocoa, chocolate, sugar, preserved milk): rationalization of the current harmonization directives replacing them by directives under the 'new approach', confined to essential requirements

— Protection of livestock: replacement of the existing directives laying down very strict standards for the protection of laying hens, calves and pigs by minimum rules

ANNEX II

LIST OF SUBJECTS ON WHICH GREEN OR WHITE PAPERS, NOT NECESSARILY LEADING TO LEGISLATION, WILL BE PREPARED IN 1993

— Guarantees and after-sales services,

— Access of consumers to the courts,

— Mobile communications and frequencies,

— European dimension of education,

— Security of information systems,

— Community initiatives (structural operations),

— Civil liability for damage to the environment.

ANNEX III

PRINCIPAL LEGISLATIVE PROPOSALS ALREADY MADE BY THE COMMISSION AND STILL PENDING BEFORE THE OTHER INSTITUTIONS

1.		CITIZENS' RIGHTS
2.		PROMOTING BALANCED AND SUSTAINABLE ECONOMIC AND SOCIAL PROGRESS
21.		**An area without internal frontiers**
211.		Ensuring the smooth operation of the Single Market
2111.		Free movement of goods
2112.		Free movement of persons, freedom of establishment and legal environment for business activities
2113.		Free movement of services
2114.		Free movement of capital and payments
2115.		Competition policy
2116.		Interoperability of network systems
2117.		Consumer protection
212.		Common commercial policy
213.		Common agricultural policy
214.		Common fisheries policy
215.		Common transport policy
22.		**Increasing economic and social cohesion**
221.		Structural activities
222.		Trans-European networks
223.		Overseas departments and territories
23.		**Stimulating growth and establishing economic and monetary union**
231.		A closely coordinated economic policy
232.		Defining a single monetary policy
233.		Stimulating economic growth
24.		**Promoting sustainable, environment-friendly growth**
241.		Environment policy
242.		Research and technological development
243.		Industry and small business
244.		Energy
25.		**Promoting a high level of employment and social protection**
251.		Social policy
252.		Vocational training

26.	**Promoting a better quality of life**
261.	Consumer protection
262.	Public health
263.	Education and youth
264.	Culture
265.	Civil protection
3.	AFFIRMING THE UNION'S IDENTITY ON THE INTERNATIONAL SCENE
31.	**Establishing a common foreign and security policy** ([1])
311.	European Political Cooperation
312.	Implementing the common foreign and security policy
32.	**Enlargement**
33.	**European Economic Area and other relations with the Member States of the European Free Trade Association**
34.	**Policy on cooperation and relations with developing countries and other associated countries**
341.	Countries of central and eastern Europe and the independent States of the former Soviet Union
342.	Mediterranean, Middle East and Gulf countries
343.	Countries of Africa, the Caribbean and the Pacific
344.	Countries of Asia and Latin America
345.	Horizontal and general cooperation and aid measures
35.	**Multilateral and bilateral relations with the industrialized countries**
36.	**Relations with international organizations**
4.	DEVELOPING CLOSE COOPERATION IN THE FIELDS OF JUSTICE AND HOME AFFAIRS ([2])
5.	FUNCTIONING
51.	**Financing**
52.	**European statistical system**
53.	**Programming and transparency**
531.	Consolidation of Community legislation
532.	Information for the public
54.	**Community administration**

([1]) Second pillar (Title V of the Treaty on European Union).
([2]) Third pillar (Title VI of the Treaty on European Union).

1. **CITIZENS' RIGHTS**

    — European Human Rights Convention: Community accession — Pending

    — Protection of personal data: ensuring that the processing of such data follows the same principles and is handled in a similar manner in all the Member States — Pending

    — Right to vote and stand in local elections in the Member State of residence — Pending

2. **PROMOTING BALANCED AND SUSTAINABLE ECONOMIC AND SOCIAL PROGRESS**

    21. AN AREA WITHOUT INTERNAL FRONTIERS

    211. **Ensuring the smooth operation of the Single Market**

    — Vocational training for national officials dealing with indirect taxation: four-year Matthaeus-Tax programme (1993 to 1996) to prepare officials for the new task of applying correctly the new tax rules entailed by the internal market and to establish administrative cooperation, in particular to eliminate distortions of competition between the Member States and to combat fraud — Pending

    2111. Free movement of goods

    Veterinary matters

    — Fish diseases: introduction of Community control measures — Pending

    Animal feedingstuffs

    — Animal feedingstuffs: particular nutritional objectives — Pending

    Plant health and quality of plant products

    — Plant health: introduction of the principle of Member States' financial solidarity and responsibility — Pending

    Technical and legal matters

    Prevention of new barriers

    — National technical standards and rules: tightening the current Community notification procedure (Directives 83/189/EEC and 88/182/EEC) to ensure greater transparency of action at national level and to improve discipline in the event of common action — Pending

    Health protection

    Pharmaceutical products

    — New medicinal products: establishment of the European Agency for the Evaluation of Medicinal Products in the context of a procedure for Community authorization to place on the market — Pending

    — Other medicinal products for human use: introduction of a decentralized procedure for Community authorization to place on the market — Pending

    — Veterinary medicinal products: introduction of a decentralized Community procedure for authorization to place on the market — Pending

    — Active and non-active medical devices: harmonization of national regulations to protect patients' and users' health and safety as regards marketing and use — Pending

    Foodstuffs

    — Labelling of foodstuffs: amendment of Directive 79/112/EEC — Pending

- Foodstuffs: assistance to the Commission and cooperation by Member States in scientific examination — Pending

- New foods and food ingredients: harmonization of the rules on production, placing on the market and labelling — Pending

- Agri-foodstuffs: harmonization of national rules for protection against contaminants — Pending

- Irradiation of foodstuffs: rules for control of foods and food ingredients treated by ionizing radiation — Pending

- Additives allowed for use in foodstuffs intended for human consumption — Pending

- Agri-foodstuffs: hygiene rules applicable to animal and plant products — Pending

Environmental protection

- Emissions of volatile organic compounds resulting from the storage of petrol and its distribution from terminals to service stations: stage 1 in the standardization of terminals to reduce photochemical emissions — Pending

Safety protection

- Certification: affixing and use of the CE mark of conformity for industrial products with a view to harmonizing the current labelling provisions under the 'new approach' and laying down a harmonized basis for future technical developments in the Community — Pending

- Approval for placing explosives on the market: introduction of a Community control system to replace controls at internal borders based on mutual recognition, on the basis of harmonization of the conditions for placing on the market to take account of essential safety requirements — Pending

- Personal protective equipment: approximation of the laws of the Member States, amending Directive 89/686/EEC to meet essential safety requirements to protect the health and safety of users — Pending

- Electrical equipment for use in potentially explosive atmospheres: harmonization of minimum safety rules for protective equipment and systems intended for use in potentially explosive atmospheres — Pending

- Recreational craft — Pending

- Lifts: replacement of Directive 84/529/EEC — Pending

- Machinery: second amendment of Directive 89/392/EEC — Pending

Taxation

- 18th VAT Directive (a): eliminating distortions of competition resulting from transitional measures introduced by the Sixth VAT Directive, with a view to limiting derogations from the VAT system as regards the VAT base and moving closer to the principle of a uniform base — Pending

- VAT on second-hand goods, works of art, antiques and collectors' items: common rules to eliminate the risk of distortion of competition and double taxation — Pending

- VAT on passenger transport: new rules amending Directive 77/388/EEC to prevent distortions of competition in road and waterway transport and eliminate border controls necessitated by the payment of VAT on transport services — Pending

- VAT on gold: common rules to eliminate market distortions and controls, by exempting transactions relating to gold for investment purposes in such a manner as to avoid disturbance to the market — Pending

— 12th VAT Directive: expenditure not giving rise to deduction	Pending
— 22nd VAT Directive: arrangements for small and medium-sized firms	Pending
— Eighth VAT Directive: tax-free allowances for travellers from non-member countries	Pending
— Excise duty on fuels of agricultural origin (bio-fuels) common rules for reduction as part of the energy, agricultural and environmental objectives	Pending

2112. Free movement of persons, freedom of establishment and legal environment for business activities

Ensuring freedom of movement for employed persons

— Freedom of movement for workers: removal of remaining restrictions on movement and residence within the Community for workers of the Member States and their families, by means of amendments to Regulation (EEC) No 1612/68 and Directive 68/360/EEC	Pending
— Posting of workers for the purpose of providing services: coordination of national laws with a view to establishing a nucleus of imperative minimum protection rules	Pending
— Application of social security schemes to employed persons, self-employed persons and members of their family who move within the Community: amendment of Regulations (EEC) No 1408/71 and (EEC) No 574/72 to remove obstacles inherent in social security schemes to the freedom of establishment and freedom of movement of persons who are not workers or members of their family	Pending
— Coordination of national social security rules: extension of Regulations (EEC) No 1408/71 and (EEC) No 574/72 to all insured persons not yet covered: non-employed persons, students and civil servants subject to a special scheme	Pending

Company law and company taxation

— European company (SE): creation of a statute as a specific legal framework enabling companies established in different Member States to merge or to form a holding company or a common subsidiary whilst avoiding the legal and practical constraints resulting from 12 different legal systems	Pending
— European company: rules to supplement the SE statute concerning the status of workers, defining the concept of employee participation and setting out several potential participation models	Pending
— European cooperatives, European mutual societies, European associations: creation of statutes with a view to facilitating the transnational operations of such bodies	Pending
— European cooperatives European mutual societies, European associations: rules to supplement the statute concerning the role of workers in each of the three European entities to be created	Pending

– Arrangements for companies to take into account losses sustained by their permanent establishments and subsidiaries situated in other Member States: harmonization of rules on compensation	Pending
– Interest and royalty payments between parent companies and subsidiaries in different Member States: introduction of a taxation scheme entailing elimination of all withholding at source	Pending
– Company structure: fifth Directive concerning powers and obligations of public limited companies, including worker participation	Pending
– Company structure: 10th Directive on cross-border mergers of public limited companies	Pending
– Tax arrangements for the carryover of losses: harmonization of Member States' legislation	Pending

Intellectual and industrial property

– Community trade mark and Trade Mark Office: creation with a view to facilitating companies' search for markets at Community level based on the establishment of a single Community trade mark system with a single application to a Community Trade Mark Office	Pending
– Plant breeding: creation of a European plant-breeder's right with a view to increasing the productivity of agriculture by promoting the constant creation of improved plant varieties	Pending
– Biotechnological inventions: approximation of the laws of the Member States concerning legal protection with a view to promoting future research in this field	Pending
– Legal protection of databases: common rules to protect the intellectual property rights of the creators of databases as well as to prevent the extraction and unfair re-use of their contents	Pending

Public procurement

– Public works contracts: amendments concerning technical adjustments	Pending
– Public supply contracts: recasting of existing instruments to consolidate contents and align them on works and services instruments	Pending
– Public service contracts: coordination of award procedures with a view to their extension to hitherto excluded sectors (water, telecommunications, transport, energy)	Pending

2113. Free movement of services

Telecommunications services

○ – Voice telephony: establishment of a regulatory environment for the activities of the providers of services	Pending

New technologies and information technologies

Standardization

– Terminal equipment for satellites: approximation of Member States' legislation for mutual recognition of conformity of terminal equipment of broadcasting stations not connected to the telecommunications networks, extending the scope of Directive 91/263/EEC	Pending

— Mutual recognition of licences and other national permits for telecommunications services: introduction of a single Community licence and creation of a Community Telecommunications Committee	Pending

Transport services

— Internal transport of goods by road: definitive cabotage system entailing the opening up of the national markets to non-resident operators	Pending
— Charging of transport infrastructure costs to heavy goods vehicles: establishment of a provisional framework for the imposition of minimum rates of tax accompanied by the possibility of introducing non-discriminatory charges on motorways to be replaced by a definitive tax system based on the principle of territoriality	Pending

Financial services

— Bank deposit guarantee schemes: coordination of national rules so as to introduce a comprehensive system of legislation based on a single licence and prudential supervision by the Member State in which the bank has its registered office, replacing the recommendation of 21 December 1986	Pending
— Reorganization and winding up of insurance companies and credit institutions: coordination of laws, regulations and administrative provisions relating to institutions operating in more than one Member State	Pending
— Investment services in the securities field: coordination of rules with a view to facilitating the freedom to provide services in this field by means of a single approval procedure and common rules on prudential supervision	Pending
— Investment enterprises and credit institutions: capital adequacy ('committee procedure' aspects), aiming at the setting of a minimum initial capital and the definition of a common framework for the surveillance of exposure	Pending
— Capital adequacy of investment enterprises (and credit institutions) to ensure that the exposure of such enterprises is subject to closer control in the Single Market: addition to the proposed directive pending on investment services	Pending
— Funds collected by institutions for retirement provision (group insurance): coordination of laws, regulations and administrative procedures relating to the freedom of management and investment	Pending
— Cross-border stock exchange listing: amendments to Directive 80/390/EEC to allow such listing without a new prospectus having to be published	Pending
— Supervision of credit institutions: measures to strengthen and clarify the role of auditors in the light of the analysis of the implications of the BCCI affair	
— negotiations with non-member countries on the exchange of information	Pending

Audiovisual services

Regulatory aspects

— Copyright: accession of Member States to the Berne Convention for the protection of literary and artistic works (1971) and the Rome Convention on the protection of performers, producers of phonograms and broadcasting organizations (1961) to guarantee authors and performers a minimum level of protection by helping to combat piracy of works, in particular audiovisual works	Pending

— Copyright and neighbouring rights: coordination of certain rules applicable to broadcasts, especially by satellite and cable, by establishing the legal and economic bases necessary for European creative activity in the cultural field	Pending
— Copyright and neighbouring rights: harmonization of the term of protection of copyright and neighbouring rights to remove the divergences and obstacles arising from the shortcomings of the Berne and Rome Conventions in this respect	Pending
— Data protection: general directive	Pending

Technological aspects

— Standards for satellite broadcasting of HDTV signals: action and support plan for 1992 to 1996 aimed at establishing a critical mass among HDTV services using European standards, increasing the number of high-quality networks and increasing the volume of high technical quality programmes	Pending

Audiovisual production

— High definition television (HDTV): encouragement for the European audiovisual programme industry (16:9 format and HD)	Pending

Energy services and products

— Exploitation of geographical areas for prospecting, exploration and extraction of hydrocarbons	Pending
— Electricity and natural gas markets: second phase of liberalization to ensure the free movement of electricity and gas and freedom of establishment for undertakings active in these sectors	Pending

2117. Consumer protection

— Time-share contracts: introduction of rules to put an end to abuses by ensuring that consumers have the necessary information before signing contracts and allowing them a set period during which they can withdraw	Pending
— Unfair terms in contracts: approximation of national rules on unfair terms in contracts between a consumer and a professional, whether in the public or the private sector	Pending
— Distance selling: establishment of a nucleus of general rules regardless of the means of communication used	Pending
— Cosmetics: revision of the legislative apparatus (sixth amendment of Directive 76/768/EEC)	Pending

212. **Common commercial policy**

— Cultural objects unlawfully removed from the territory of a Member State: rules on return	Pending
— Export controls on certain dual-use (civil and military) goods and technologies and certain nuclear products and technologies: introduction of a Community system free from the obstacles associated with national controls	Pending

- Checks for conformity of products imported from third countries: introduction of product-safety rules — Pending

- Community trade protection instruments: harmonization and rationalization of decision-making procedures, by transferring areas currently in the Council's jurisdiction to the Commission's — Pending

- Common arrangements applicable to imports from non-member countries with market economies and State-trading regimes: removal of remaining national restrictions, standardization of the various import arrangements, simplification of formalities to be completed by importers and adjustment of decision-making procedure by transfer of areas currently in the Council's jurisdiction to the Commission — Pending

- Community procedure for administering quantitative quotas: establishment of a Community procedure replacing the current system for splitting Community quotas into national shares, to prevent market fragmentation — Pending

- Tariff and statistical nomenclature and the Common Customs Tariff: new rules introducing greater consistency into the system of codes and facilitating computerization of customs procedures — Pending

213. **Common agricultural policy**

- Bananas: establishment of a common market organization, replacing the various national arrangements with a system designed to guarantee adequate supplies for consumers and ensure disposal of Community bananas — Pending

- Potatoes: common market organization — Pending

- Forestry: renewal of Regulation (EEC) No 1615/89 establishing a European forestry information and communication system, for the coordinated implementation of measures for the conservation and development of forests in a way which is compatible with rural development and the conservation and improvement of the environment — Pending

214. **Common fisheries policy**

- Controls on fishing activities and landings: introduction of an improved integrated global control system to replace Regulation (EEC) No 2241/87 — Pending

- Implementation of the common fisheries policy in the Mediterranean: harmonization of certain technical measures to establish a common system for the management and conservation of fishery resources specially suited to the region — Pending

215. **Common transport policy**

Economic measures and regulations

- Shipping: positive measures — Pending

Harmonization measures

- Computerized reservation systems for air services: harmonization with a view to improved competition between carriers and better customer information — Pending

- Air traffic management equipment: short-term integration and harmonization rules — Pending

External matters

- Carriage of passengers and goods by road: negotiations with certain non-member countries — Pending

22. INCREASING ECONOMIC AND SOCIAL COHESION

221. Structural activities

- Cohesion Fund to finance environment and transport infrastructure projects of common interest: temporary instrument — Pending

- Cohesion Fund to finance environment and transport infrastructure projects of common interest: establishment — Pending

- Greek islands in the Aegean: programme of targeted actions to reinforce structural assistance and to introduce special measures to improve the supply of agricultural products and develop local products — Pending

222. Trans-European networks

- Declaration of European interest: introduction of mechanism to mobilize private funds to finance trans-European networks — Pending

- Transport infrastructure programmes for 1993 to 1997; amendment of Regulation (EEC) No 3359/90 — Pending

- Road networks, inland waterways and combined transport: Community master plans — Pending

23. STIMULATING GROWTH AND ESTABLISHING ECONOMIC AND MONETARY UNION

233. Stimulating economic growth

- European Investment Fund: creation, as part of a growth initiative, of a fund to guarantee investment in the public and private sectors and facilitate the financing of small firms — Pending

24. PROMOTING SUSTAINABLE, ENVIRONMENT-FRIENDLY GROWTH

241. Environment policy

Horizontal aspects

- 'Eco-audit' (evaluation and improvement of environmental performance): Community master plan for information for the general public to promote utilization by industry of the most effective environmental management systems, including eco-audits, and encouraging the use of reports certified by accredited environmental auditors — Pending

Air

- Global Community strategy to stabilize CO_2 emissions by the year 2000, to promote energy efficiency and to improve security of supply:

    — monitoring mechanism for CO_2 and other greenhouse gas emissions — Pending

    — introduction of a CO_2/energy tax to encourage consumers to save energy and switch to cleaner energy sources — Pending

    — improving energy efficiency (transport, construction, industry) under the current SAVE programme — Pending

    — alternative energy programme (Altener) 1993 to 1997 — Pending

    — Climate Change Convention — Pending

- Reduction of air pollution by emissions from light commercial vehicles: approximation of the laws of the Member States to make emission standards as strict as those applicable to passenger cars under Directive 91/441/EEC — Pending

- Reduction of air pollution by emissions from passenger cars: approximation of the laws of the Member States with a view to a further reduction in limit values from 1996, by amending Directive 70/220/EEC as last amended by Directive 91/441/EEC — Pending

- Emissions of certain pollutants into the air from large combustion plants: amendment of Directive 88/609/EEC — Pending

- Sulphur content of gasoil: amendment of Directive 87/219/EEC to introduce stricter limit values with a view to reducing emissions from ships, motor vehicles, heating plant and industrial installations — Pending

Waste

- Supervision and control of shipments of waste within, into and out of the Community: replacement of the rules introduced by Directive 84/631/EEC to take account of the implications of the Single Market, and requirements flowing from the Lomé IV Convention and the Basle Convention — Pending

- Damage caused by waste: introduction of the principle of the civil liability of producers — Pending

- Packaging and packaging waste: common rules to prevent and reduce the quantity of packaging waste, to promote recovery and reuse and to reduce final disposal to the strict minimum — Pending

- Incineration of dangerous waste: introduction of measures and procedures to prevent or minimize harmful effects on human health and the environment — Pending

- Landfill of waste: harmonization of environmental and technical standards to protect soil and groundwater and prevent the occurrence of contaminated sites — Pending

Contributing to the protection of human health

Nuclear safety

- Basic safety standards to protect workers and the public from the dangers of ionizing radiation: revision of Directive 80/836/Euratom — Pending

- Shipments of radioactive substances within the Community: transitional measures pending entry into force of the new basic safety standards — Pending

Contributing to the prudent and rational use of natural resources

- Convention on international trade in endangered species, wild flora and fauna (Cites): revision of Regulation (EEC) No 3826/82 — Pending

Developing international cooperation (follow-up to the June 1992 Rio Summit)

- Montreal Protocol on substances that deplete the ozone layer: conclusion — Pending
- Basle Convention on the control of transboundary movements of hazardous wastes: ratification — Pending
- Convention on biological diversity: conclusion by the Community to allow it to participate in a global legal instrument in support of environmental objectives and the aims of many sectoral policies — Pending
- Convention on climate change: negotiation by the Community to allow it to participate in a global framework for cooperation on sustainable development, in relation to transport and energy in particular — Pending

242. Research and technological development (R&TD)

- Third framework programme of research and technological development (1990 to 1994): additional funding — Pending

Developing international scientific and technical cooperation

- EEC-Australia: negotiation of an agreement on scientific and technical cooperation — Pending

243. Industry and small business

- Intensifying growth-oriented priority measures for enterprise policy, in particular for small and medium-sized enterprises: multiannual programme (1993 to 1996) — Pending
- Ensuring the continuity of enterprise policy, in particular for small and medium-sized enterprises: multiannual programme (1994 to 1997) — Pending

244. Energy

Promoting energy efficiency and new and renewable energy sources

- Altener programme for the promotion of alternative and renewable energy sources: new series of measures for 1993 to 1996 — Pending

Nuclear energy

- Euratom safeguards: amendment of Regulation (Euratom) No 3227/76 to strengthen the international safeguards and non-proliferation arrangements — Pending

Coal

- New Community rules for State aid to the coal industry with a view to restructuring the industry to take account of social and regional imperatives — Pending

External aspects

- EAEC-Russia: Agreement — Pending

25. PROMOTING A HIGH LEVEL OF EMPLOYMENT AND SOCIAL PROTECTION

251. **Social policy**

Employment and pay

- Atypical work: introduction of minimum rules for different types of employment contract to eliminate distortions of competition and to improve transparency in the labour market — Pending

- Atypical work: introduction of rules to improve the working conditions of part-time workers with regard to vocational training, information and social security benefits — Pending

Improving working and living conditions for workers, so as to make possible their harmonization while the improvement is being maintained

- Organization of working time: introduction of minimum rules covering rest periods, conditions for the use of shift work and the protection of health and safety, to help firms adapt to changes on the labour market — Pending

- Protection of young workers: adjustment of national labour regulations applicable to workers so that their specific development, vocational training and access to employment needs are met — Pending

Improving health protection and safety at the workplace by harmonizing conditions while maintaining the improvements made and by the gradual application of minimum rules (through individual directives within the meaning of framework Directive 89/391/EEC)

- European Agency for Safety and Health at Work: establishment — Pending

- Protection of workers on means of transport: minimum requirements — Pending

- Protection of workers on board fishing vessels: minimum requirements — Pending

- Protection of workers against risks related to exposure to biological agents: minimum requirements implementing Community rules and regulations on biological agents — Pending

oo - Protection of workers against risks related to exposure to physical agents: minimum requirements on exposure to noise, vibration, optical radiation, magnetic fields and waves, etc. — Pending

Promoting the information and consultation of workers

- Information, consultation and participation of workers: introduction of rules for the establishment of a European Works Council in Community-scale undertakings or groups of undertakings for the purposes of informing and consulting employees — Pending

Ensuring equal opportunities and equal treatment at work

- Reversal of the burden of proof in the area of equal pay and equal treatment for women and men — Pending

- Parental leave: granting of leave to either parent to encourage the sharing of family responsibilities — Pending

- Social security: complementary measures to resolve the problems raised by current directives in areas including widow's/widower's pension, family allowances and the same retirement age for women and men — Pending

Combating social exclusion and encouraging the integration of persons excluded from the labour market

- Economic and social integration of the disabled: third Community action programme Helios II (1993 to 1996) to promote the development of a coordinated Community policy — Pending

		– Transport to work of workers with reduced mobility: minimum requirements to improve mobility and safe transport to work and thereby facilitate the occupational, economic and social integration of the workers concerned by gradually adapting and redesigning means of transport	Pending
26.	PROMOTING A BETTER QUALITY OF LIFE		
261.	**Consumer protection**		
		– Health and physical safety of consumers: establishment of a Community system for the rapid exchange of information on products which fail to conform to Community or national rules and could compromise the health or physical safety of consumers	Pending
		– Home and leisure accidents: establishment of a Community information system	Pending
262.	**Public health**		
	Preventing disease, with particular reference to the major scourges and drug addiction		
		– Action against drugs: creation of a European Drugs Monitoring Centre and a European information network on drugs and drug abuse	Pending
		– Tobacco advertising: introduction of a ban on advertising to reduce the number of smokers	Pending
263.	**Education and youth**		
	Promoting cooperation with non-member countries and international organizations		
		– Tempus trans-European mobility programme 1994 to 1998: assistance to the countries of central and eastern Europe in the area of university studies, and extension to include the independent States of the former Soviet Union	Pending
264.	**Culture**		
	The audiovisual sector is covered in section 2113		
265.	**Civil protection**		
		– Prevention of industrial disasters: negotiation and conclusion of an international convention within the International Labour Conference	Pending
3.	**AFFIRMING THE UNION'S IDENTITY ON THE INTERNATIONAL SCENE**		
31.	ESTABLISHING A COMMON FOREIGN AND SECURITY POLICY		
33.	EUROPEAN ECONOMIC AREA AND OTHER RELATIONS WITH THE MEMBER STATES OF THE EUROPEAN FREE TRADE ASSOCIATION		
		– European Economic Area: adjustments to the Agreement	Pending
34.	POLICY ON COOPERATION AND RELATIONS WITH DEVELOPING COUNTRIES AND OTHER ASSOCIATED COUNTRIES		
341.	**Countries of central and eastern Europe and the independent States of the former Soviet Union**		
		– EEC-Russian Federation and other members of the Commonwealth of Independent States which belonged to the former Soviet Union (Ukraine, Kazakhstan, Uzbekistan, Belarus, Azerbaijan, Tajikistan, Armenia, Kyrgyzstan, Moldova, Turkmenistan) and Georgia: agreements for cooperation and partnership in the fields of trade, economics, politics and culture and proclaiming the principles of the CSCE and the Helsinki Charter	Pending
		– EEC-Commonwealth of Independent States of the former Soviet Union and Georgia: Tacis programme of technical assistance for economic reform and recovery	Pending

	— EEC-Lithuania/Latvia/Estonia: conclusion of trade and cooperation agreements	Pending
	— Efficiency and safety of nuclear facilities in central and eastern Europe and the independent States of the former Soviet Union: financial contribution to the improvements programme by means of Euratom loans	Pending
	— EEC-Slovenia: negotiation and conclusion of an economic and trade cooperation agreement, including an agreement on transport and a financial protocol	Pending
	— EEC-Albania: extension, with a guarantee from the Community budget, of assistance from the European Investment Bank for Albania under the cooperation agreements	Pending
342.	**Mediterranean, Middle East and Gulf countries**	
	— EEC-Turkey: signature of the Fourth Financial Protocol	Pending
	— EEC-Syria: conclusion of the Fourth Financial Protocol	Pending
	— EEC-Morocco: negotiation and conclusion of a Europe-Maghreb type agreement to establish an association with Morocco	Pending
	— EEC-Gulf Cooperation Council: negotiation and conclusion of a free trade agreement	Pending
343.	**Countries of Africa, the Caribbean and the Pacific**	
	— Common organization of the market in bananas: establishment of a specific support scheme for the traditional ACP supplier countries	Pending
344.	**Countries of Asia and Latin America**	
	— EEC-Central American isthmus: negotiation and conclusion of cooperation agreements	Pending
	— EEC-Andean Pact countries: negotiation and conclusion of a cooperation agreement	Pending
	— Latin-American banana-producing countries: establishment of a diversification and development fund	Pending
	— EEC-Association of South-East Asian Nations (Asean): negotiation and conclusion of a new economic cooperation agreement	Pending
345.	**Horizontal and general cooperation and aid measures**	
	General cooperation measures	
	— International Cocoa Agreement: renegotiation (production policy, pricing, financing system)	Pending
35.	**MULTILATERAL AND BILATERAL RELATIONS WITH THE INDUSTRIALIZED COUNTRIES**	
	— Temporary admission of goods: conclusion of the Istanbul Convention for the consolidation in a single international instrument of existing conventions to facilitate international trade	Pending
	— Textiles: renewal of the Multifibre Arrangement and of bilateral agreements with Taiwan and the Republics of former Yugoslavia	Pending
5.	**FUNCTIONING**	
51.	**FINANCING**	
	— Financial perspective 1993 to 1999: draft Interinstitutional Agreement	Pending

	– Risks faced by the Community budget: creation of a Guarantee Fund containing provisions to cover these risks should Community guarantees on loans to non-member countries be activated	Pending
	– Budgetary discipline: renewal of Decision 88/377/EEC of 24 June 1988 to take account of the reform of the common agricultural policy and the new functions of the monetary reserve and to provide the necessary legal bases in the budget for guarantees on loans to non-member countries and emergency aid to these countries	Pending

Measures to combat fraud

	– Protection of the Community's financial interests: new rules repealing Regulation (EEC) No 1468/81 designed to facilitate access to information obtained under the arrangements for mutual administrative assistance between the Member States and the Commission and to extend cooperation in combating fraud in the customs sector and in agriculture	Pending

52. EUROPEAN STATISTICAL SYSTEM

	– Framework programme of priority activities in the field of statistics 1993 to 1997	Pending
	– Transit and storage: statistics relating to trade in goods between Member States	Pending
	– Economic statistics: common nomenclature of products by means of the statistical classification of products by activity in the Community (CPA)	Pending
	– Statistical units for observation and analysis of the production system	Pending

Transport

	– Road accidents: establishment of statistical system	Pending

Business

	– Business register for statistical use: establishment	Pending

Research and development

	– Multiannual programme for the development of statistics on Community R&D and innovation in order to set up an integrated information system in this field	Pending

53. PROGRAMMING AND TRANSPARENCY

531. **Consolidation of Community legislation**

	– Wheeled agricultural or forestry tractors or machines (Directive 74/150/EEC, etc. 24 directives and 33 amendments)	Pending
	– Doctors (Directive 75/362/EEC, Directive 75/363/EEC amended four times, Directive 86/457/EEC)	Pending
	– Public procurement	Pending
	— works contracts (Directive 71/305/EEC amended five times)	
	— excluded sectors (Directive 90/531/EEC amended once)	Pending
	– Fruit juices (Directive 75/726/EEC amended three times)	Pending
	– Fertilizers (Directive 76/116/EEC amended three times, Directive 77/535/EEC amended three times, Directive 80/866/EEC, Directive 87/94/EEC amended once)	Pending
	– Dangerous substances and preparations: marketing and use (Directive 76/769/EEC amended 12 times)	Pending
	– Units of measurement (Directive 71/354/EEC amended three times)	Pending
	– Fisheries (Regulation (EEC) No 3086/86)	Pending

Joint declaration on the 1993 legislative programme

The European Parliament, represented by the Enlarged Bureau, and the Commission, in the presence of the Council:

having regard to the need for swift ratification and effective implementation of the Treaty on European Union,

having regard to the Commission's work programme for 1993, presented by its President to Parliament on 10 February 1993,

having regard to the work programme of the Council Presidency for the first half of 1993,

having regard to Rule 29a of the European Parliament's Rules of Procedure,

having regard to Parliament's resolution of 10 March 1993 on the legislative programme for 1993,

having regard to the measures which the Commission plans to submit to the Council within the time-limit envisaged in its legislative programme (COM(93) 43 final),

1. Confirm the importance of better programming and coordination between the institutions, to improve the effectiveness of the Community's decision-making process as well as transparency *vis-à-vis* its citizens (Declarations of Birmingham and the Edinburgh European Council);

2. Welcome the new approach adopted by the Commission in its presentation, which is more consistent and clearer in its objectives, and the indication of:

   (i) measures which could give rise to prior consultations with the other institutions and with the representatives of the economic and social partners,

   (ii) proposals for the consolidation of legislation during the current year,

   (iii) policy discussions which the Commission intends to conduct during the year (White Papers, Green Papers),

   (iv) international agreements to be negotiated and concluded by the end of the year,

   (v) measures it intends to put forward within the new pillars of foreign policy and cooperation in justice and home affairs;

3. Approves the legislative programme with the addition of the measures listed in paragraph 4 and the document programming its work which each institution is to implement as part of the legislative process;

4. Agree to act as appropriate in the following areas:

   (i) proposal on the right of residence for students,

   (ii) communication on energy policy,

   (iii) report on the application of the directive on equal treatment for self-employed men and women,

   (iv) implementation of the pilot stage for student mobility,

   (v) further consideration of the rules on comitology in order to achieve greater transparency;

5. Confirm their commitment, as a matter of priority, to the following principles:

   (i) measures to aid recovery and combat unemployment,

   (ii) strengthening and implementation of the single market,

   (iii) preparations for EMU,

   (iv) cooperation with third countries,

   (v) democracy, transparency and subsidiarity in the Community decision-making process;

6. Call on the Council to adopt as soon as possible the proposals on the implementation of the Community Charter of the Fundamental Social Rights of Workers and on worker participation as well as the proposals for a European company statute and a European cooperative society;

7. Believe that, pending the entry into force of the Maastricht Treaty, work should continue on a European industrial policy and a policy on asylum, immigration, visas and security checks to catch those in possession of drugs;

8. Undertake to inform each other as soon as possible of any changes envisaged as regards any new initiatives and any timetable changes; the Commission undertakes to submit its proposals in good time and Parliament undertakes to deliver its opinion as quickly as possible;

9. Undertake to revise the Interinstitutional Code of Conduct with a view to ratification of the Treaty on European Union;

10. Confirm the mandate of the Interinstitutional Coordinating Group to continue its work of exchanging information, monitoring implementation of the legislative programme and solving any technical problems arising;

11. Decide to forward the legislative programme and this declaration to the other institutions and the governments and parliaments of the Member States and to publish them in the *Official Journal of the European Communities* for public information.

European Communities — Commission

Address by Jacques Delors, President of the Commission, to the European Parliament on the occasion of the investiture debate of the new Commission

The Commission's work programme for 1993-94

The Commission's legislative programme for 1993

Joint declaration on the 1993 legislative programme

Supplement 1/93 — Bull. EC

Luxembourg: Office for Official Publications of the European Communities

1993 — 69 pp. — 17.6 × 25.0 cm

ISBN 92-826-5358-7

Price (excluding VAT) in Luxembourg: ECU 6